One Manner of Hunger or Another

Bill Johnston

Poet Warrior Press

Special Thanks

To my editor Danny Cerullo
To Laura Galaviz for the cover art
Many thanks and love to Kate Bailey for cover design
and layout
To Nick Guzman, Amy Miles and all of the Concrete
Seas
To Anthony Rocco Sclavi for original cover design
To Joan Barbara Simon for moral support from the UK
To my sister Liz for the marketing funds
and every single one of my friends and family for
listening me talk too much about this book for nearly a
year

Thank You All

The Fish That Sings Clearly

Blasting a hole in my skull was the first impulse. It was a quick brutal end that left little to the imagination. After a visit to the corner gun shop where I found buying a gun harder than the second amendment led me to believe, I wandered next door passing a tempting dice game and the smile of an old whore into the liquor store and found an alternate finish, row upon row of shiny bottles and striking labels calling out to me to take them on a little trip to my final destination, into a final darkness. The price for a firearm of adequate caliber to end me cost considerably more and the idea of drinking myself down the drain followed by a hangman's knot seemed more fitting, I hadn't the will to finish myself in such a drawn out manner at first, but I'd always liked to drink and thanks to my time as a boy scout a length of rope would suffice.

The room looked like hell. The walls were off yellow with brown stains emerging from behind faded paint. There was a small sink in the corner below a broken mirror. The bathroom was down two flights of stairs and shared between the other unfortunates who found their lairs within the run down tenement.

The only furnishings were a four legged folding table with a sticky brown surface in the center of the room, a rusted metal folding chair, and a stained twin mattress I'd salvaged from the dumpster of a Goodwill against the wall by the door.

Then what I deemed, at first glance upon, renting the room as my final companion.

It was not golden with flowing fins or swimming within a tall circular fish bowl. It was only the size of a large minnow, with large eyes that stuck out from both sides of that ugly little head and resembled something you'd place upon your hook instead of one of the elegant aquatic creatures that grace aquariums. Even a proper fish bowl was lacking as the creature lived in clear, glass cereal bowl. I noticed immediately that the fish swam not randomly back and forth between the walls of its glass home but directly towards me. No matter where I stood within the room there the fish swam; it pressed itself against the glass, its two bulging eyes focused upon me.

Not sure when the last time it had been fed was and confident that it hadn't much time left as my roommate. I decided to let it go hungry as I had so many times, and that after a few days its gills would cease to pulse and it would float upon the surface. I decided that when the little finned bastard turned belly up in its bowl I would take that as my queue to leave the world I currently occupy and venture out to see what else remained at the end of a rope hung from the ceiling. I paid very little attention to my only companion at first.

Unaware of just how much time I had left, I began to drink. There was no joy involved in pouring the alcohol down my throat. I drank the cheapest bottles of vodka in the store, large clear plastic bottles that slowly formed a pile in the corner of my shitty little room. I threw them back, one swallow following another, until the world around me grew fuzzy, and the room grew comfortable, and I awoke the next morning laid out upon the filthy mattress with no memory of lying down.

I lost track of the days spent alone in my room, staring at the fish as it swam ever towards me. The passage of time I deduced by adding up the empty vodka bottles in my room as I had neither clock nor window by which to judge a night's passing. I drank more and more as time passed before I fell unconscious and had no idea how often I ventured out to visit the liquor store a block away to be met with the light of the day or the glow of a street light completing my pilgrimage weighed down with bottles.

I ate little while waiting for my roommate to die only consuming a few slices of bread a day to soak up the vodka and sustain my unwanted life.

Funds ran low. The vodka I'd been purchasing, though cheap, began to eat away at what little of my money remained from renting the room, and my last companion, the cursed little bug eyed guppy that never seemed to cease pressing it's nose less face against the glass, ever swimming at me, had not seemed to falter after several days without food.

I had fish as a child that died without warning though I cared for them well. The ending to this story was taking far too long. I often drank calmly fondling the orange extension cord I had fashioned into a noose to hang myself from the exposed boards of the ceiling. I'd had enough. With less than twenty dollars in my pocket and only left with one quarter of a bottle of vodka for the night, I reached a decision.

I swore quietly at the gilled little bastard and matched his gaze with mine as I emptied the last of the vodka down my throat, and, with only a grunt, I swiped my annoying little roommate, bowl and all, from the table and smiled as it shattered on the tiled floor. The water spread around my feet, the glass settled, and the fish flopped upon the floor, flipping from one side to another, gills working frantically, eyes bulging as it began to dry.

I felt quite satisfied. I smiled as the little fucker suffocated feeling that as he had spent his last day upon the earth ...…so would I.

Then the fish began to sing. I was stunned for a moment, sitting in disbelief. I gave a quick manic laugh. It had finally happened. I had finally lost it, achieved the madness that had been teetering over me for so long. My only comfort was that I would not have to endure it. Had I planned on living much longer, I would have been terrified.

It started slowly and I was unsure as to the source. The sound soared both high and low at once. The fish craned its head from the ground pumping it's lipless little mouth, opening and closing, and the sound was unmistakably one that had never been heard by any ears upon this planet. The walls shook from the bass, reverberated, and struck me from all directions. It was as if I had heard the sound from not only the ears upon my head but from within and I clutched the arms of my chair and leaned back as the sound flowed through and around me.

I knew then that I had been blessed to experience something that defied description. I knew then that I heard the fish sing.

The sound ceased slowly as the fish lowered its head to the ground and its gills stopped pumping death.

I have never acted so quickly, with such purpose, in my life.

I dove to the floor as the fish ceased to move. Swooped it from the ground with both hands and rushed it to the sink.

I turned both knobs of the sink and plunged the fish into the water as it filled the basin, swearing softly and looking down at its lifeless body. Then, slowly, the gills began to work, the mouth opened and closed and I released the living fish into the filling sink.

I did my best to fill the sink with water both not too hot and not too cold and was relieved to see the fish swimming in my filthy little sink. After flipping about for a moment it brought its head to the surface of the water and began to swim, once again, towards me, pressing its head and bulging eyes against the walls of the sink.

I stood drunkenly watching the fish swim against the wall of the sink and was no longer quite sure of what had occurred. So I laid down upon my filthy mattress to gather my thoughts.

My eyes reopened hours later. I could not recall where or who I was. I looked up from the piss smelling mattress at the ceiling slightly lost when reality, if it could be called such a thing, returned to me. My head was pounding. My tongue was a dried hunk of flesh in my raspy mouth. I rose from the mattress groggy and crossed the room, dismissing the fuzzy recollections of the night before when I pressed my foot down upon a jagged piece of glass.

In an instant my memories returned and I walked, as fast as one can with a piece of glass in one's foot, to the sink.

My beloved pet was swimming happily within. All at once I felt I'd regained a dear friend.

I took to speaking to the little fish, feeding it bread crumbs and praising its beautiful song. I even went so far as to panhandle on the street to acquire enough change to buy a glass so that my angelfish wouldn't have to sit all day in a dirty sink.

I did not return to the liquor store.

It occurred to me that what I had experienced that night could have easily been some form of hallucination. That did not concern me as much as the fact that the memory of that voice began to grow soft.

I tried to play the sound in my mind as one does a nursery rhyme before going to sleep but it only grew fainter and fainter.

So, after some time, I reached within the glass holding my only friend on this earth and I plucked it into the deadly air, tail between my thumb and finger and waited.

Its gills pumped death and it flopped back and forth, but soon it only wriggled slightly, and, against my every instinct, I held it pinched against my palm. I held it and watched as it went limp, the lids on its beautiful eyes closed and it ceased to be my companion and became merely a dead piece of fish.

Pinching my friend's lifeless tail between my thumb and fore finger I raised him up, tilted my head back, and dropped him into my mouth swallowing him whole.

I took a moment of silence for my final companion, stood upon my folding chair, looped the noose around the exposed boards of the ceiling, and, with the song of a fish in my mind, kicked the chair out from under me.

If death wasn't so painful and slightly easier to bring upon oneself would any of us grow old?

Before the weight of my body splintered the

exposed beam in the ceiling, everything had begun to fade. My vision grew fuzzy and the entire world grew distant. It was as if I was wrapped in warmth napping while my reality withdrew, the volume decreasing and my vision growing faint. Of course there was the feeling of increasing tightness around my neck, the instinctual kicking of my legs and swinging of my arms, the screaming for air that anyone who has ever held their breath too long knows of, and the unavoidable panic that I imagine only the most disciplined of monks could avoid.

However for a moment, let's call it a moment anyway, I have no idea how long I hung, for a moment I welcomed calm, black silence that I had hoped would last an eternity. Nothingness.

The concept had always eluded me. I had always envisioned dark, infinite space, or sleep, or a state of mind brought into being by a trance. But I lacked the ability to grasp it entirely.

Indescribable, yet wholly encompassed in one word. Nothingness.

My throat was raw. My ass spoke in the touch of thousands of pricking needles, but my leg had the most to say about how I was treating my ragged undernourished body.

I suppose I was lucky I didn't break anything in my journey hanging from the ceiling to the destination of crashing to the ground. I had been unconscious long enough for my ass to fall asleep just enough to let me know that it had lost circulation but not enough to actually go numb. My leg had taken the brunt of the fall and had twisted beneath me, and of course there was the bruise wrapped like a tendril around my throat.

It hurt to stand and the mirror confirmed that my appearance would be one of, for a while at least, a man that had just wrapped an extension cord around his neck, hung it from the ceiling, and kicked a chair out from under him.

Not to worry. I had never really bothered with appearances, not my own anyway. In retrospect that may have something to do with my current situation but there may be time for that sort of contemplation later. For now it was due time to go outside and throw myself from the curb into the fastest moving bus I could find. I briefly considered being run over by something more common, like an SUV, but there was no real way to ensure that the airbags would deploy properly and I had no intention of hurting anyone but myself. It's not like I was completely out of my mind or anything.

I limped from the front door of my building, stepped over a man sleeping on the sidewalk that may have stolen my shoes from me while I was sleeping some time ago, and headed down an alley to the nearest bus stop.

They always had a game of dice going in the neighborhood. It just so happened that on this night they had put one together in this alley. It just so happened that on this night as I passed them I slipped my hand into my pocket and found a wadded up dollar bill I had neglected to spend before my death. It just so happened that I liked to gamble.

I had forgotten about my appearance until I saw the looks on their faces as I approached holding the dollar bill before me. I hadn't bathed, hadn't so much as stood in the rain, for weeks at least. I had been living on nothing but white bread and vodka for as long as I could manage, I limped, and I had clearly been strangled.

There were three of them. The one holding the dice was a big guy in black with a dark complexion to match and a scar shaped like a crescent moon on his chin. The man on his left was shorter with lighter skin and looked like he had just gotten off work in his black slacks and button up stained white shirt. The third fellow was shorter, white, and the least well dressed in a blue t-shirt and baggy jeans, with a smile that revealed brown broken teeth, though he put the expression away when he saw me.

They stopped just long enough to mutter a "what's up?" and discern that I had no chance of disturbing their game. I came close enough to almost join their half circle rolling dice on a brown piece of cardboard against the wall of a building.

My leg began to hurt more with every step so I leaned against the wall; dollar bill clutched in hand, and watched my three new friends bet, roll, and exchange words along with their money.

I was fully intending to pause long enough for my leg to ache less, throw the dollar down, roll the dice, and walk away penniless to find a busy street, when I began to feel something.

It rose within me slowly, an almost imperceptible feeling and sound. A slight movement within as one would feel a tremor in one's chest. A slight sound one would hear just on the edge of auditory capacity. It rose within me and then grew leaving me with a feeling of elation and with no doubt as to the nature of its sign. Jesus had not experienced such a feeling even at the time of his resurrection. No noise of this nature could be written upon a page. Hearing angels sing in comparison would be a disappointment. Any concoction of chemicals known to neither man, nor deity's nectar squeezed from her own breast, nor orgasm ever experienced would suffice.

I heard the fish sing again and I knew. I knew. This man was going to roll a seven.

The song hit me hard. I snapped to attention with my hands clenched in fists at my side and my head all the way back and shared a laugh with the sky. A laugh saturated with desperate joy and release.

As my acquaintances looked up from their game to meet me with odd looks I stepped, limp forgotten, to the cardboard gaming table and placed my wadded up dollar bill onto three comparably clean singles, nodding at the looks given me and between them alike and smiled.

As the dice finished their clatter seven dots smiled back at me from white cubes.

To say the dice rolled in slow motion would be cliché. In truth the rest of the night seemed to move quickly. The game went on for another hour or so and two more times I felt the fish sing and placed my bets and two more times I swiped my money from the ground and clutched it to my chest as if it were dear to me. It didn't occur to me until later that I was lucky that my companions had lacked hostility. That they hadn't simply decided to take their money back and maybe throw in a light beating for intruding on their game, but they had pity.

Pity being one of the only things I was accustomed to receiving I was glad to take it.

It never occurred to me to seek out the bus stop again.

I returned to my room. I had only paid enough rent for one more night. It didn't matter. I would not be staying there long anyway.

The key to winning when you gamble is to lose. Even the biggest high roller can be asked to leave if their game is too good for a casino. Win too often with a bookie and he'll refuse to take your bets. Avoid illegal games if possible and, when playing in one, show caution in your winnings. You never know when the black jack dealer or the game owner will decide that they're better off just kicking you out and keeping the money. They might even leave you with a few bruises and a broken arm. It's not like you can go to the police and tell them someone took thousands of dollars from you while gambling illegally in the basement of Chinese food restaurant can you?

Winning, anyone who's ever pawned their watch on a wild weekend in Vegas can tell you, is a good problem to have.

Some people count cards. Some people rehearse tossing dice on their own crap table in their attic. Some people cheat in teams using signals at the poker table or spend years studying the patterns of slot machines. I rely on the supernatural tones of a fish I swallowed on a bender in a crummy motel room just before attempting to hang myself with an extension cord.

My first bets consisted of everything I had. The odds did not matter. I felt the grip of the song and laid down all the money I had. Soon I had more than I had ever seen, which isn't saying much, but once my winnings began to accrue I bet less, lost enough to avoid suspicion, and began to buy the kind of life I never thought I could have.

I rented a condo. I purchased a relatively new luxury car. I began to buy things that I did not need, a flat screen television with every channel that I never watched, a black leather sofa with matching love seat, the largest bed I could fit through the doorway to my room. I walked into stores and plucked things from shelves at whim never bothering to look at the prices. I visited the ATM just to walk down a street pulling the largest bills from my wallet and dropping them to the people I passed who called that corner their home.

I spoke to no one besides the bookies and a passing comment to cashiers in casinos and at the track. I had no phone; there was no one to speak to. I had no friend I'd see at the bar, no family to ask me to dinner. I had only money.

I spent a lot of time sitting quietly in my well furnished home. I would lie on my overpriced furniture in a stillness of mind, of environment, of body; I would simply sit comfortably and exist. Breathing clearly and reveling in the mere state of lacking a struggle.

It took more time than one might have thought it, but I grew bored. I would turn on the television flipping channels until I grew frustrated that it failed to lift my malaise. The rush I felt gambling began to fade. Betting became tiresome. Being aware of the outcome of a bet began to lack appeal, and the less I needed the money the less I cared.

The song within, though still effective, no

longer had such a strong grip. At first it had held me tightly in ecstasy, had me clenching every muscle in my body, laughing outwardly, caressed my mind in joy. However its strength very slowly withdrew and I was of a mind to either avoid situations that tended to trigger it in an attempt to ration it out, or seek to immerse myself within what remained. To wallow in its grip like a hog.

I began to pace the hall of my condo and having conversations, though I was the only one in the room, I knew I needed something to shift my focus.

The aquariums were delivered the next day at extra expense that I cared nothing about. The tanks were filled, checked for the right temperature and acidity, and the fish were carried in two at a time in clear plastic bags bulging with water.

Before the day's end I had cleared away every surface in my home to allow placement of my new friends and the television was placed in my closet. I was surrounded by the blue green reflection cast from the glass and the brightly colored movement of my new companions' tails, the pumping of their gills, and their endless swimming.

Learning to care for my pets was a welcome distraction and after naming them, feeding them, and staring quietly at them for a time, I set out to fill the one bowl that had been left empty in my home. I set out to find the closest thing to the fish that I had swallowed whole so long ago and gifted me with everything I had, including my life. I set out to find a reminder of my savior.

I drove to every pet store and aquarium I could find. The pet stores were unhelpful and though I knew the aquarium fish were not for sale I wandered from tank to tank patiently seeking out every fish. Hoping that upon finding my guppy every last cent I had would be enough to scoop him from the tank and bring him home.

My search was a futile one and I began to wonder if the minnow I had swallowed and been blessed by was the only one of its kind. I lay in bed picturing the fish for fear that I would lose its image from my mind before ever seeing one again when a thought occurred to me.

I waited impatiently outside the bait shop for nearly an hour before the owner flipped the sign in the window to "OPEN" and unlocked the front door.

I brushed passed the man and walked to the back where there were rows of rectangular tanks filled with minnows and instantly saw it. Pressed against the wall of the tank, eyes' bulging, swimming towards me, was my ugly little friend. If I had not swallowed him whole personally I would not have been able to tell the difference.

I continued betting when my funds went low and spent my time staring at my minnow as it swam ever towards me in its large round bowl until one day I came to a decision that handing out money to random street dwellers was not enough. That I would use my time and relative wealth to help the people with whom I had shared a home for so long. I would, at the very least, feed the homeless.

I began stocking the larders of a local homeless shelter I had waited in line at many times when sleeping in the streets. I brought as much food as I could fit into my car at least once a week and, depending on the state of my winnings, they ate well. The first day I arrived with a carload of food had been the first day the shelter had ever served steak.

I almost walked right by her. Leaving the soup kitchen after a resupply I glanced down at her as I passed but didn't pay her much notice. I had been living well long enough to not feel the sting of familiarity with the bums and vagrants I passed, and had grown into no longer looking at this side of my past. Her tattoo, however, caught my eye. It was no wonder I didn't recognize her. Her hair, which had once been a light red was so encrusted with filth that it appeared a clump of black and brown and she lay motionless propped against the wall, head hanging heavily on her chest.

We had shared moments. We had shared moments I had never shared before or since. We had shared anything the other had for a time, held each other through cold nights, and been the only ones who gave a damn about either of us. One day she had not returned to our temporary home of cardboard and plastic bags and I had not seen her since.

I leaned down, spoke her name softly, and lifted

her off the pavement and across the street to my car.

I carried her into my home and took her straight into my bathroom. I stripped her layers of filthy clothing off and laid her into the tub.

She had lost weight since I'd last seen her and she had been thin even then. Still she was familiar to me, her tattoos, her body, but there was the addition of track marks on her legs and arms and a few more scars than I recalled.

When I turned the water on from the shower head she opened her eyes and smiled slowly, but recognition was not there. I sat on the edge of the tub and leaned in, holding her gently, and whispered my name in her ear. I had no doubt my appearance had changed since we'd last seen each other, the weight gained and regular shaving served as an effective disguise, but after a moment her smile grew, her eyes lit, and she pulled me toward her with the combination of a giggle and a shriek.

We held each other there for a time, while the water poured over us and the grime of living in the street turned the bathtub brown as the water went its course down the drain. She whispered a command then and I was happy to oblige. I lifted her from the tub and carried her into my bedroom, throwing her on the mattress and began to take off my wet clothing.

She giggled again as she undid my belt and pulled my pants and we rolled over each other kissing and grasping at one another.

I didn't think I would ever make love to a woman again. Even with the car and the condo I didn't have the confidence, the respect for myself that I assumed a woman required, and I was not willing to pay.

The song began as her legs parted and I awkwardly placed myself between them and grew as I placed myself within her. I did not take long and as I climaxed so did the crescendo within, and, as I spent myself, I felt the song move. It moved quickly from it grasp upon my chest and mind down through my torso and out of me. As I gave what I had to offer to her so did I give the song. As the song left me I knew. I knew.

I could feel the song within her. I knew then that I had a child with the only woman that I ever loved in any way. That I had given that child the only thing I had ever owned worth receiving. I had given that child the song.

When I awoke the next day it occurred to me how little I actually knew of the mother of my child, how I had others to provide for now, and how certain I was of the fact that the rather lucrative occupation of gambling I had before was now not an option.

I spent the next two days in a variety of activities that I had long ago grown unaccustomed to. I began to attempt to get to know this girl I had brought into my home, though conversations were something I had not experienced in a while. I began to search the classifieds for work, and I began to look forward to the rest of my life.

On the morning of the third day I put on the nicest suit I owned, pulled a hundred dollar bill from my otherwise empty wallet, placed a note mentioning where I'd gone along with the money and several take out menus on the night table beside which my love was sleeping, and went out to find the first decent job I ever had.

I returned over four hours later after handing in several resumes, sitting through two interviews and coming to the realization that I had little marketable skills. The thoughts of the state of my unemployment fell quickly away.

The living room was dark and silent. I stepped quickly through the hall straight into my bedroom and found her there lit with the fading sun through our bedroom window.

She lay motionless in one of my t shirts on her back, eyelids open with no sign of pupils. Her mouth lay open as well, filled with yellowish foam that ran down one cheek. Her arm hung from the bed, with the needle still sticking from her vein, and the belt still strapped loosely to her forearm, and so you will find her and me.

And so this brings you up to date my readers. It took me longer than I thought to complete my suicide note. Though I've tried to be brief, forgive me for waxing poetically from time to time. As nearly my last act I may have delved too deeply at parts and left you wanting more from others but I find my hands sore from my too tight grip upon pen, and I have no more patience for the written word, though I do doubt that any of you will ever believe it.

Simply know that as my last act I plan to follow my beautiful love with the pressure placed upon the blunt end of a syringe. Know that the worst thing that awaits me, as well as awaiting you, is most likely...

Nothingness

Sincerely,

A switch is a simple mechanism.

On, off, the connection of current with the flick of a finger.

Who among us understands how a switch works? Many, but who among us could build one? This number is smaller.

The device which I wrote this poem upon is merely a series of switches, binary code that stretches before you pulsing and flipping between zeros and ones. A switch is a simple mechanism, but to line a thousand of them before you and to learn to read every possible combination of this array is not so simple.

Who among us understands how a computer works? Now the numbers begin to thin, and who among us could build one? A show of hands would leave mostly empty air.

What impresses me is how much we rely on these switches to function. What amazes me is that most of the time they do.

Your mind is a series of switches, neural pathways that pushes energy through grey matter at the speed of thought.

And what is the speed of thought?

The electricity that pushes through your brain is composed of electrons that have the potential to move at the speed of light. Your every breath, twitch, movement, everything you are is guided by electrical impulses that flash through your mind at a speed which cannot be exceeded

As the last line was read energy was being pushed through pathways in your mind flashing from one point to another and allowing yourself the luxury of thinking about how you feel about what was just read.

It is true that we have reached a level of understanding of nearly everything which has never been seen, from a subatomic particle, to our own bodies, from the chemical reaction of the sun that keeps our planet warm, to the chemicals released by your brain at this moment

We are many things. We are complicated creatures. We own prejudice. We are destructive.

Still I am proud of every single one of us that has ever lived

Every single time I flip a switch.

Bukowski

looking at a man like that makes me say many things to
myself

should've fought more

should've drank more

should've been more than usual

should've

and then I think of the word

should

and go to my fridge for a beer

My meal was a bone complete with a side of teeth marks

An evening's entertainment was finding the marrow had long ago dried up

I was thankful that though I still starved they had thrown me a bone

The cell left me just enough room to sit with my back against one wall and my toes pressing against the other

Though I would have liked the room to pace I'd spend my mornings grateful that I had even the room to take the weight from my feet

The light goes out when the sun ceases to shine through my window no larger than a loaf of bread, but this light helps me keep the time. I tell myself that there are others with no light at all.

I crawl with the lice that are my companions, however at least I have companions. I would pluck myself bare, one hair at a time, face, body, and head, but then I would have no company. Then I would not be able to eat. Then I would not spend my days choosing the bugs that are unworthy and leveling my disapproval upon them.

I gave up screaming and pleading with the shadows that crossed the light that shines in the gap beneath my door, but I have myself to banter with. At least I still have a voice to emit. At least I am still capable of hearing.

There is only me to talk to, but I have found I am a skilled conversationalist.

Yes my cell gets very cold, and I have nothing, not even rags, to hold my warmth to me, but on those nights I shake head to foot the exertion involved is my only exercise. I still have both of my arms to wrap around myself. I still live to feel the chill of every night.

They told me I would never leave this tiny cell. They told me I would receive no mercy. I have found mercy in that I am still alive to suffer, because things could always be worse.

I will always have myself until a time when I no longer have anything.

Comedy of errors

not long ago I was diagnosed with schizophrenia

yeah crazy huh

they prescribed all kinds of medication

depakote

clozapine

lamotrigine

mostly drugs that rhyme

and I sat at home all fucked up on medication for quite some time

until one night I realized that no matter how many times I cleaned my glasses the warning on the labels still said that it would cause blurred vision

so I talked to my doctor and I asked him if all this medication was really necessary

he said, "oh well, the white one is to get you going in the morning, the green one is to settle you down for the evening and the other one is to help you sleep for the night."

and I thought to myself he sounds just like the guy who used to sell me coke, pot and beer in high school soon after, a good friend asked if I thought it was such a good idea to go off medication and I told him look as long as you spend your time hanging out in the right side of my brain you'll have to respect my decisions

I've been through some hard times, and I'm often misunderstood, but

like I told a buddy of mine at a party not long ago, I said "you know I'm not really an asshole I'm more of just a jackass, um what was the question again?"

One of my uncles asked me once what I wanted to do for a living and I said I wanted to understand, he said "understand what?" and I said "everything"

he just laughed and said "good luck!"

good luck

I will never forgive him for that

wishing me good luck

I blame him when I'm sitting up high at three in the morning trying to get shit off my mind and it occurs to me that all of the world's happiness is based solely on saturated fat

I suppose I would never have written these words without his encouragement.

Whether or not that is such a good thing is entirely up to you.

Pissed

I walk into a bathroom stall, take out my dick, and just as I'm ready to release my knees buckle. The toilet bowl comes toward me as I collapse.

I'm curled around the toilet bowl and the floor begins to fill with water.

I cringe from the cold water soaking into my clothes, but after a moment I accept that I'm soaked and the water on the floor rises to several inches.

I cling desperately to the rim of the bowl and strain every muscle to bring myself back to my feet.

When I wake up, I really have to piss.

Pinnacle

Pushing ever upwards

to reach that point,

that peak,

the highest point in your mind.

Two steps forward

one step back,

driving always upwards,

with every step you rise higher

loosening the footing behind you,

sending tiny avalanches in your wake,

causing more damage

to those that have chosen similar paths

yet remain further behind,

and one day,

someday soon,

you will reach that point,

and find,

that the highest peak has no footholds,

no shelter,

and is crowded with those

who

cling.

The Belt

The first time my dad sent me to fetch his belt,

I came back with a tie.

Everyone laughed and all was forgiven.

The second time my dad sent me to get his belt,

I came back with a tie.

No one laughed.

The lizards seek heat from the sun rock hot spots

The golden haired blue eyed girls find their joy in the
men that bring laughter and those with the flat stomachs
and chiseled faces, those who fit the bill reap the
benefits and find themselves with kids that would
repeat the formula,

the young and confused and those that question the
nature of things turn to chapels and wise men and
science and the thoughts of those that thought well, they
seek to stand upon the backs of the thinkers while the
statuette hold fist to chin and ponder, we are lucky that
some men of such thought have existed and the children
of those that thought well hold upon the electrical
impulses that flash from point to point in their minds
and their muscles,

what they placed upon the luck of the well bred now
fall to the arrangement of the double helix and the
points in which they meet and soon will pay top dollar
to arrange not by god but by the bidder to model their
unborn protégé,

to oil the car we oil the beach, and upon the beach we
scrub the pelican clean and release it to its grainy black
surroundings stinking of gas stations and jiffy lubes,

I am proud to claim many a man friends that bring you
the food, clean the table and mop your footsteps from
the linoleum, we are not yet what is spent in action for
the given forty hours a week, give or take, and there are
those among us who are in agreement and there are
those among us who would gladly receive the given

accolade but mainly the doctor, the lawyer, the educated middle to upper class not the busboy, the dishwasher, the man who raises your garbage can once a week and asks that you bag your boxes before placing them in a container beyond your concerns,

personally I would rather spend the dollar to leave me be, to exchange the money for the concerns that surround me, sleeping in until the sun almost sets is a commodity that can be more expensive than the simple passage of time may portray,

the kind man may label one unique, may label one eccentric and pinpoint the talent, the potential that they may find in an individual but those of the thought may also say that there is found weakness within said being that therein is found the lazy, the dumb, the incompetent and I am found among them, not merely the weak but also those of thought,

the smashing of one's own head or fist against the wall is cliché among the angst ridden, amongst the sterile white halls of the ward, amongst the race known as human yet we all recognize its origins, it's beginnings and ends, we all feel the need to strike outward and within and do so acceptably but only as long as we do without the scarred wrists, the battered partner, and too frequent empty bottles and coke vials and damaged property,

we gauge the success of the time spent on many things we cannot take with us, for in actuality what can we take with us? What can we claim to bring to the table at the very last hand? What can we bring? The pyramids? The generations and names of slaves and the unfortunate that have served beneath us?

I would like to believe that the greatest of our current life that may compensate us in death is the sorrow and presence of the ones who knew, an account of the joy we've brought, of the burdens we've shouldered for those that we could, for the good, but isn't therein also an account of the backs we've whipped? of those that we've climbed past on the great ladder, of those whose importance in life we've placed beneath us, of those who perished building our tombs and whose children have done the same,

To believe that the cycle of our lives is much like that of condensation is to have the concept of what is likely true, we begin long ago above the earth and fall upon it singularly and in groups, we fall upon the earth and gather together to form communities large and small over time we carve out our own in the stone, in the mud, fortunate enough to find purchase, we carve out what we can as naturally as we flow from one location to another, and in the end we are consumed by conditions, consumed by life, consumed by the elements, consumed until the heat of existence returns us to the sky to gather and cool and fall below once more, and in most incidents of life we are no more aware of it than the rain is aware that it is wet, or the snowflake that it is unique.

Unsaid

Have you ever been quietly sitting in a room

full of people,

sociable atmosphere,

actually feeling good about yourself,

about the people around you,

about everything,

till someone turns to you and says,

"don't talk so much"

Time

is merely the method

in which organisms of higher intelligence

clock their own decay.

These Invincible People

I cannot comprehend how they do it

These invincible people

who work sixty hours a week

who arrive home

wash their dishes

walk the dog

who still hold smiles on their faces at the end of the day

who still ask their children how they are at night

who read them stories

before going to bed for four hours

only to get up and do it all again

Even those that drink until the sun rises

And when they awake an hour later

they drive to work still drunk and sweat away the
hangover

they never seem to mutter to themselves or think
repeatedly

how they must quit this job

how they must rest their bruised feet

Where do these people keep their sorrow?

Where can I buy such strength?

Merely claiming my existence

To breathe every day I struggle

These invincible people surround me

Perhaps I am not willing to pay their membership fee

Perhaps I do not possess what they carry with them

to and from work

into and out of bed

Perhaps it takes years to gain such momentum

It's a present I'm not sure I want to receive

I may be incapable of not weeping upon ripping the
paper from this gift

Surely the world would crumble without these invincible people

Surely I ride upon their backs

As even my greatest efforts seem, in comparison, of great sloth

They make me look bad

these invincible people

And at times I feel they are the sled dogs being whipped by lesser mammals

While I would prefer to stay off the trail entirely

to freeze to death

These invincible people burn as a flame in the dark

And these invincible people cannot help but light my way

We had come to see grandpa.

After wandering down identical

sterile white hallways I found

myself squinting up through

fluorescent lighting at one of

the doctors, "Your grandfather's

dying" a pause "do you know

what death is?" I often reflect

on what answer he could've

possibly given, had I not responded

with a muted

"yeah".

We made it a scavenger hunt.

There were a lot of items on the list, dirt, crayons, eggs, motor oil.

We gathered all the necessary items, piled them together, and proceeded to dump them all in the neighbor's pool.

We hadn't been getting along.

Psych-Kilt

I'd spent a few weeks in the psych ward.

My dad came to visit me in a kilt.

I had to explain to all the other patients why my dad showed up in a skirt.

A sermon on the mount for a bunch of people, one man telling others to be nice to one another was a novel concept, they thought, kneeling to the ground seems more than a little symbolic the ground beneath our feet being more of a solace to some than the deity dreamed up in our minds and grown like plaque building within the arteries and passage ways within the pumping muscle in our chests,

Faith is found in statues of those who suffered in a notably historical manner leaking fluid from the ducts within their stone eyes. There are those who placed knees to floorboard and faith to the accidental occurrence of one resurrected man or the mother that bore him without the seed of a father seen by some who look too closely. Why would a miracle occur to you in the wooden grain of your closet door, the water stain of a rundown home or the peeling paint of a long decrepit billboard?

the final days have come and gone and will be labeled once more only to be passed over by the shadow of those who realize that this last day has lasted many passages of sun and moon and will not be so predictable as to be labeled on the calendar, that the final rise of the sun will be predicted by those who seek science with lenses and tubes and count the breaths of earth along with the desiccation of a species that none of us have ever seen or the temperature of a fault line or the gravitational pull of a dot in the sky,

When NASA places the end date, when the nations of earth call on us one and all to embrace each other in our last minutes, hours, days, and nights, then I will empty my bank accounts of the little worthless money that is left and clutch at life's existence that remains,

with all remaining fingers, toes, arms, legs, and chest, then I will hold most dearest every breath that can follow another, then I will celebrate like no being has, then I will speak to friends, family and god of my every love, fear, and all that rests between. Every last one of us will speak to one another as one does in the wake of death one with sincerity and in a flowing outpour of everything every one of wants to say to every other person for the final time. The world will be our deathbed. Death will unite life in a moment, one great flash, rather than circumstance and time greeting us with the end individually.

There are gods within my reach that I can attest the existence of. For instance, the god of madness, all but the unlucky ones bow to this creator of unique existence, for no man is insane in exactly the same manner and those who've known its touch, its breath upon their face, those attest to insanity's power recognize it's mark upon others that it keeps gripped closely to its ribs, madness strikes as death in that it holds no favorites to its condition, there has never and will never be a being that lies out of reach of the condition of a unique mind,

that is the status of the existence of god, gods, or enlightenment. A unique status, for no matter how many come together to speak of, or listen to, or experience the existence of their faith or fear or love it is all a unique mindset

We may agree on a beginning, middle, and final example of religion or what is holy and find ourselves so mentally in sync that we lie united in our frame of mind however all that remains is our perception drawn in through the holes in our faces and the sensations wrapped in skin, in this way we are alone, in this way we are connected, in this way we know nothing yet nothing remains to be known.

April Fools

It was April Fool's day.

Me and Nick decided something must be done.

We tied a rope around his waist and hung him from the stairwell with a sheet around his neck.

When his mom came home she didn't even blink. She walked right past him hanging there by the door.

"You know one day you really will hang yourself Nick" she said.

An important lesson was learned.

Do not fuck with Nick's mom.

At what time did you decide to live?

At what time did you realize you exist on the whim of many, some of which you have never met?

What was the day, year, decade that you reached acceptance of your family, job, the aching in your chest, or the loneliness you feel when surrounded by those you love

When did you grip tightly that morning moment of clarity as it all comes back to you and squeeze it until the juices run down your knuckles and lick the nectar to break your morning fast

How many times have you turned your view of things, gazing at them from every direction until you know them as something new although you've always known them well?

How many times is enough?

There is never and always a time for a new way

There is always and never a time to breathe, inhale, exhale, and take a moment before pressing on

I ask you for time but I will not receive it

You ask me for time and it is something I cannot give

Time the drive to work

Time the first kiss

Time for others

Time for yourself

Do you have something that does not exist?

Do you have something that always has?

Do you have the time?

Something Within

It is known as energy, it is known as strength, it is
known as my life

We know this force as well as we know ourselves and
so some of us are fairly unaware of it

It compelled me to write these words, it compelled me
to share them with you

When there is no wrong there only remains a lack of
agreement

When acceptance comes you see that dissent between
others is inevitable

Dissent will always be

When dissent flows through and around you, you must
deal with it as one does with a freezing night air

You must let it pass around you, shield those you can
from it, and seek shelter wherever it is found

It is okay to react in your way in the same way it is
okay to grow cold in a chilling breeze

The sun will rise. The weather will change. The
summer will always come again.

To be led by the hand is fine, but be prepared for that

hand to be empty and yourself to be slightly lost

To forge ahead alone is much vaunted but prepare to turn around one day and find others unable to follow your trail

We can walk together guiding each other from stumbling over the obstacles hidden in tall grass

We belong to each other, for even someone who has never met another human being still has it in him to be alone

I belong to all of you so please care for me as best you can

And I will care for you

What's On Your Mind Old Man?

We need the wisdom of the starving old man sitting in
the mud in his grass hut with only one tooth you can
always see because he's always smiling

Others may follow your footsteps

Your trail may have begun where another's has ended and join or cross many other roads

Your trail may never see another traveler

Your trail may seem extraneous, even useless, when compared to the paved marked highways that you run beside

All this is inconsequential

It can never be said the path you make is anything but your own be it footsteps in the mud for merely several feet or a walkway that covers the world

Every inch, every marking, every grand stone bridge, pothole, or rotted wooden handrail belongs to you.

Carve the deepest, widest, farthest path one can

This is the most

All

One can do in life

My brother was the oldest of the brothers, and me being the second youngest male we conquered a lot side by side. Painting. Landscaping. Every task that required the man of the house fell to my brother and every task required someone to help.

That someone was me.

We once had to clean out the shed in the yard where we stored all the garbage before it was hauled away.

When we stepped into the shed, armed only with rags around our mouths and under our arms and cans of cleaner, we faced maggots covering walls and floors.

Every step was marked with the sound of the crunching of these maggots carpeting the wooden floor.

There was instantly and understandably a loss of morale and I looked my brother in the eye as our faces fell at the task we were about to undertake and I smiled and said "I step on fortune cookie."

So it has always been with my brother and I. Me supplying the clever remarks and smiles and him supplying the majority of sweat.

We laughed then. As we always have. And we sprayed and wiped every maggot from the floors and walls of that shack only to see it torn down a month later.

We had a government funded house and I had never recalled a time when we could afford to run the heat.

We had a woodstove in the basement and lacked wood to heat the house, sometimes lacked the wood to heat even the one room. So all five kids and my mother would pile upon the mattress next to the stove in our warmest pajamas with the padded feet worn thin and a pile of blankets, and that is where and how we would sleep.

But fire goes away. Wood burns away. And blankets are pulled away from you in your sleep.

This often happened to us and me. Being the smallest I slept atop all the rest of my family and in the cold darkness, I would freeze.

I would curl into a ball and shiver, and as I began to freeze I would mutter to myself the reality of the night I faced

"Cold. Cold. I'm so cold." I would mutter this repeatedly until my body gave in and I slept or the sun rose and warmed the room and it was time to dress and go to class.

One night my teeth were clacking together and I had assumed my mantra, and while everyone slept my brother awoke and shook me from a chilly trance and asked me "Are you cold?"

Every night after he would ensure me the thickest blanket and many nights after until spring he would awaken in the middle of the night to ensure I still had it.

I do not have many things on this earth to this day but I

still have a brother that does not want me to be cold.

Futile Eloquence

Idly twirling thoughts around my fingerprints

Perpendicular from the ideal state of mind

Suddenly eloquence dribbled from my mouth

Bled from my fingertips

I stood upon its shoulders

It pushed me from the edge

Held me gently by the throat

Traded with me question after question

The exchange of words were erotic

However there was no climax

The words grew soft

We grew tired of their use

A shower was taken

A television switched on

A night ended

I drive a red rusted out car everyday

I cannot replace it for I have not the title to it and who really does?

The parts fail. The tires that bear its weight lose their tread, spring holes, and air leaks from them over time. The oil needs changing and the price to do so is minimal in retrospect but this takes time as well and who has the time to grace the waiting room with the couch and the questions and the up sell of promise garnered with more expense.

I have no mechanic I can trust, but the car squeals in torment at every turn.

I add fluids to the car daily, checking them with care, I add fuel as well, and though I clean it when it grows cluttered it is long overdue to be cared for thoroughly, and I am afraid there is no one left for such a task, and I am afraid I lack the will for anything but maintenance.

This car is my life in many ways. Without my rusted red car my life would not be the same. It could be said I would have little life left.

Though it has more years and less mileage than I, I hope to leave this world behind before it, because then there will be less to mourn.

I know the words mean nothing

And that nothing can mean an awful lot

I know that footsteps ring louder when heard alone

And that being alone has its own steps

I know that to scratch always brings more itching

And that to heal one must itch

I know the mind is infinite

And that we've already seen it's limits

I know that we face incalculable experiences

And that the act of experiencing is a single one

I know that the will can crush

And that it takes less to crush one's will

I knew that ignorance brought bliss

And never thought I'd opt for stupidity

I knew that I would love

And yet never thought I'd receive so little in return

I once knew the meaning of being busy but happy

And have since lost that to a still complacency

I knew that the pills would change my emotions

And, that since, my emotions have changed about the pills

I knew that there was always something to ask myself

And that now I request that I stop asking

I know that the air we inhale is ours

And what we exhale is for god to breathe

I know that the ground beneath my feet is mine

And yet I have never owned it

I know that sleep is a necessity

And that I opt between wanting it always and wishing I could go without

I know that I know nothing

And that one day
I'll have answers to questions we don't have

Or I won't have any questions at all

Friends for Sale

I'm not sure how my father met them.

They had a big two story home. It was a very nice place.

They were a married couple with a young girl.

We shared a little two bedroom apartment

There were six of us, two brothers, two sisters my father and me.

They appeared to be a very happy family.

They would serve dinner and were very generous.

They'd give us bottles of shampoo and dried soups, anything that seemed to draw our interest.

One day they received an Amway magazine in the mail. They sat down and went over every page commenting on how nice it would be to own this or how that was such a good deal.

"Oh we need to order an American flag" or "Look at this."

It occurred to me one day that we hadn't seen them in quite some time so I asked my father what happened.

"He basically told me that if I didn't buy Amway from them we couldn't be friends."

Looking back I can see that the time spent with them was as much a sales pitch as a dinner party.

Looking back I can't imagine that my father had not recognized the same, with them giving away or discussing every little thing they'd bought through Amway.

Looking back we still ate their food and enjoyed the evening, and took home everything that was offered.

Now I ask you. Who was taking advantage of whom?

Group Therapy

Shortcomings passed around the table

Few strengths and many weaknesses

Discussing that which does not exist

Past around the table

We sit comparing gaping wounds

That would long ago have healed

If only we could keep from peeling away the scabs

Extemporaneous Appendage

Gripping on instinct.

Grasping at everything.

Clutching,

always at nothing.

I find a use for it

now and then.

It never gets a sleeve.

Who can afford a tailor

for such an

extemporaneous appendage?

Discussing Politics

A well traveled pilgrim who has never left his own
home

I seek those like me

most have yet to view their own pride as a luxury

I serve them a slice of my mind

lick the plate clean when offered one in return

a diligent host, I offer seconds

many courses pass

the meal passing through air between us

earnestly exchanging syllables

punctuating the no longer idle thought with the
occasional gesture

as the wine flows so does the pace

as our momentum strengthens

our clarity diminishes in proportion

little to nothing is accomplished

I am left with no choice but to declare our conversation

a success

Words

Most tools can be used for a variety of purposes.

A screwdriver can pry up a stone.

A saw can be used to draw a straight line

but words,

can only shape people,

and we,

we shape everything else.

I am alone

I had written it over and over on a crumpled piece of paper with a marker, and left it behind. The deed had been of far more importance than any result.

I awoke in the middle of the night with a need to write it down,

over and over.

I am alone

I am alone

I am alone

My first poem

My mom woke me up later in the night with the crumpled piece of paper in her hands. She screamed at me not to leave this type of shit lying around. That if I did it again I'd see what would happen.

I was maybe seven years old.

I did not write again for years.

The Pills Eat Me

I eat the pills

They make me

Tired

Dizzy

Light headed

Slow

Sleep too much

They make

It hard to swallow

My limbs ache

My body tingles

The pills take me

So I take the pills

Selling disfigured mannequins.

No attention drawn to an emotional wound that hasn't turned green.

Left without bandages, and lacking the sense to rip the bed sheets.

Purifying the water pumped into your toilet.

Trying to be funny when you're the only one in the room.

Looking down while thinking of a man standing directly beneath you in China doing the same.

Asking your cat for a favor.

Asking for help only from strangers.

Conducting symphonies only in your mind.

Writing letters you'll never mail to dead relatives you never knew

Opening bills you can't pay,

Sending out checks anyway.

Two hundred dollar cable bill when you ain't got gas.

Earning a poverty wage, to pay off a debt from an unattended class.

Smiling most often when you're unhappy.

Hurrying to save enough time to waste.

Seeing the weakness in every kind act.

Lacking, while eating, the presence of mind to taste.

For once asking the right question.

Forcing someone else to laugh.

Steering through life, navigated by others' advice.

Viewing people as figures on a graph.

Crying over the death of an enemy.

Disliking someone the first time you've seen them.

Suppressing amusement at a friend's pain.

Written evacuation of soul.

Verbal cleansing through a series of pre-specified sounds.

Serving you a slice of futile eloquence.

Would you like coffee with that?

Liver Failure

Everything came into focus slowly. The images began as unintelligible shapes and gradually became sharper. In the beginning I saw several outlines before me. They could have been a skyline or a tree line and they were dominated above by a pulsing, purple light. The sound came to me then. It began as merely a roaring one would hear approaching crashing waves, but then began to take the form of laughter and the all too familiar sound of many people talking over one another. As the blurred bulges before me took the shape of the back of people's heads my focus was drawn to the light over them. I was unsure whether all of this was moving towards me or I was coming closer to it, but I found everything coming together before me as if I was a mounted camera zooming into existence and my focus was being adjusted.

Everything came into frame and the focus became perfect as I stood, dumbfounded, in the shadow, my back to wall, gawking at a crowded bar with a large neon sign above it. The purple neon flashing sign spelled out "Liver Failure" over and over: "Liver Failure" pounding into my head, pulsing repeatedly against my frontal lobe in head splitting violet.

I was dizzy and chose to follow my heads momentum to see how, just how the hell, I'd gotten here. I looked left, then right, and then followed my second look to turn completely around. I stood against a wall in a bar I had never been in, alone, and had only one thought in my head. "That bar looks crowded I better get the bartender's attention."

I approached the bar, surveyed the crowd, and bellied up to it. Sadly they had not left me a stool on which to sit.

I assessed the fellow patrons.

There were two mourning, hard working, and lower class looking people to my right. They may have come together after work from the same factory or warehouse. They wore faded blue jeans and jackets worn thin at the elbows and shoulders. A dive bar like this provides sanctuary after a ten to twelve hour shift for many victims of manual labor but, besides the occasional exception, a conversation with one of these types usually consisted of how unhappy they are either with their jobs, wives, kids, or unpaid bills. Occasionally I'd spark a conversation with the outgoing enlightened laborer that would twist my view of things, spinning my ideals in his hand until I realized that happiness came from within. Of course, given that I did not drink until I could no longer recall anything but what a great guy he was, the impact of his words would fall away over the following week and leave me with only the impression of what an asshole I am for managing to be generally unhappy despite all I have. I did not see much promise in these two. Their expressions were as sour as the cheap beer they were drinking and they hunched over their drinks breathing into them, staring downward at the bar, as if their breath kept their drinks alive and the drinks in turn sustained them.

Just past the morose duo sat three women. There was nothing exceptional about two of them. They were blonde, wore earrings far too large, and wore sparkles on shirts that held unexceptional bodies. They both had too many rings on their fingers, too many acne scars on their faces, and two tramp's stamps glaring at me, one a tattoo of a butterfly the other a faded rainbow complete with the pot of gold perched just above an unpromising ass crack.

The woman sitting between them, however, was a vision. She had on tight black slacks over twin, muscular legs. A black t-shirt with a low cut neck revealed a body with proportions arousing enough to leave me with no doubt as to whether or not there is a higher power. Her eyes were the size and shape and color of almonds, her nose was held away from her face to the point of perfection, and her enticing lips rose in a smile when our eyes met.

She sat between the other two wholly unremarkable girls. They leaned into the bar to talk past her to each other as she sat up straight with a general look of disinterest that had quickly faded when she had set those eyes upon me.

Over the years I have learned that hesitation brings uncertainty. To hesitate brings doubt, perhaps not in her but in yourself, and this was a moment that would not pass by with me standing idly. I took the few necessary steps towards her with confidence and the words fell from my mouth accordingly "Hi my name's Chris can I buy you a drink? " The words met another smile, this one raised slightly at one end, and I thought surely the voice that would follow would lead me into the night of my life when the attention of the girl closest to us snapped in our direction like a flag in a strong wind. "Why don't you just leave us alone? We'll buy our own fucking drinks." I have never been met by two sets of eyes so judgmental over so little in my life while the beautiful woman's eyes merely rolled slightly and found something interesting to gaze upon on the ground. "Can't we just sit in peace for one second without some man trying to fuck us?" said the girl on far side. "Why don't you just get lost?"

The two tramp stamps turned their backs to me and remained looking firmly away. "Hey I just..." I began but there was no pulling this operation from the flames. I received three backs in response although the one of my interest did present a backwards glance and a momentarily bitten lip.

I can take a hint. Fuck this little dive bar I've always hated them. I am out of here.

The place was small. A bar with seven filled bar stools. Three filled booths to the left with a touch screen jukebox with an out of order sign taped to it to the side. Behind me was the bare wall out of which I had apparently emerged. To my left was a pool table pushed into the corner with the felt slashed diagonally across it and in the other corner was jammed with a cheap foosball table.

Where was the exit?

No. No this is silly. There must be an exit.

I took another look around. This was something I, you, have never seen, the inside of a room in which you are standing without a single doorway, nothing but smooth white walls. I turned to the working class. "Hey man" I said placing my hand on his grey and white plaid coat and leaning in. "Where is the exit?"

Have you ever asked what you felt was a stupid question and found that you are in a room full of people with the same thing on their mind?

He laughed, shook his head, turned it back towards the bar and placed it to a mug of beer. I turned to the unpleasant girl immediately to my right. "Excuse me how can I get out of here?" I said, tapping her on the shoulder. She responded by holding her middle finger up from behind. I looked up to pretty girl next to her. "Hey! Can you please tell me where the exit is?" She looked up from chewing on her lip and said nothing only shook her head slightly from side to side. "Come on! You gotta be fuckin kidding me right? Where's the door out of here?"

"Hey!" It was the bartender. He was about six feet tall with a shaved head and goatee. "Hey order a drink or get out."

"Hey man" I said "I'm not sure I can get out"

He leaned in closer over the bar and replied "I'm not sure you can get out either so order a drink already."

"Alright" I said "Give me a drink and tell me where the exit is so I can finish my drink, leave, and report you for not having a clearly marked door out of here."

"Hey man" Said the bartender whose name I noticed "Dave" was pinned to his chest. "I don't have time for this shit. Have yourself a drink. A seat will open up for you soon." His tone was both sympathetic and threatening. "What can I get you?"

"I'll have a long Island iced tea."

"We only have beer."

"I'll have a Guinness."

"You'll have beer."

"Fuck it, whatever you got."

The bartender turned his back. I glanced left and saw the stool next to me had mysteriously become empty. I looked back to the bartender to ask another stupid question when I noticed that, although he had not returned to my end of the bar a tall glass of beer had appeared before me.

I reached out for my drink and my hand began

to shake a little as I took hold of the beer. I took a sip. It was the worst beer I ever had. The tremors in my hand began to rise up my arm to my shoulder and I took a long drink of this flat, warm concoction. The tremor subsided and I sat down upon the bar stool.

"Isn't that the worst swillish horse piss you've ever drank?"

I looked to the man sitting on my left for the first time with any focus. His head was shaved and he had about a week's worth of growth on his face. He was short and stocky with a big chest and matching belly. He wore black hipster glasses, and a faded pink Floyd t-shirt. He had a crescent shaped scar on his chin and his right arm was covered in markings. They were not tattoos but appeared to be a repetition of four tiny vertical lines with a diagonal line drawn through them. They seemed to go all the way around his arm all the way to the wrist.

"Hey man" I said "where did the guy go whose seat I took?"

"I don't know. I never see anyone come in or leave. They definitely do though. I don't even know how long I've been here. Nobody has the time. There are no windows. I got bored once, one day or night, and started to count the time by the number of drinks I'd had." He lifted his right arm and pulled back the sleeve to reveal more lines tightly packed all the way to his armpit. "See?" He then lifted his shirt. The tally nearly stretched across his chest and had begun to run down to his stretch marked belly.

"The least you can do is keep your fuckin shirt on chubs!" yelled the closest tramp stamp down the bar.

"Fuck you Bethany! Why don't you go back to being a ragged fuckin' bitch?" he yelled down the bar, followed by "My name is Will, Big Will if you really feel like being an asshole about it. Welcome to hell, Chris. I'm convinced we're in some kind of alcoholic purgatory myself but nobody here seems to want to think about that." He then leaned back on his stool and shouted. "Especially that fuckin twat plug Bethany and her cunt rag friend! Not you in the middle though honey you're beautiful." He then leaned in and said "I can't seem to get a single word out of the sexy mute in the middle. I've had over three thousand drinks since I got here. I've been fuckin hammered for what must be months, that is if time even exists here, and I'm glad you're here, man. The last guy who had your seat only stopped pissing, moaning and blubbering long enough to take a drink. I swear to every god that must have sent me here there is not enough piss water in this hell to make listening to that shit bearable."

Years of drunken training kicked in and I responded to his tirade in the same way everyone should respond to a crazy drunk. I nodded slightly to whatever he said, looked away, and took another drink.

"I'm sorry man. I'm fuckin drunk. Hey bartender!" Will bellowed "How about some fuckin' coffee?"

Dave looked down the bar where he was wiping wet circles into the wood with a white rag. "You know we only have beer, Big Will. Now calm down. Don't make me get the manager."

Will's face fell as well as the tone and volume of his voice. His complexion paled and the expression on his face spoke of apologies before his voice did. "Oh no need to get the management Dave! We don't need to get the management Dave! There's no need to bother the management!" Will seemed to turn inward then rocking back and forth slightly mumbling repeatedly, "No need to get the management. Will doesn't get along with the management. I don't like the management at all."

"Hey, Dave" I asked looking left and right around me before turning my attention to him. "Just what the fuck is going on here? Come on man just tell me what the hell this place is."

Dave moved closer from behind the bar to the sink to wash a glass looked up smiled and said "Don't worry about it, Chris. Why don't you have another beer?"

"Look, Dave, I don't want another..." I began when I looked down and noticed a full beer had replaced my half full glass, "I just want to know…" I began again just as the tremors rippled up my drinking arm more strongly than ever and I found myself sipping the beer. I set the glass down and looked up to finish my question when I noticed that Dave had vanished.

"Oh well" I said out loud to myself "I'll just have one more drink then go."

I slammed the beer down, and rose from my seat at the bar. I had to find some answers. There was something very surreal about every moment of time I spent in this bar. I suppose I reacted the same way as someone walking along the street, who witnesses something so unexpected, they take a moment before properly reacting to see if anyone else on the street is bearing witness to the same spectacle ensuing before them, and so in disbelief I decided to confirm what was going on in my head synched up with the rest of reality.

Big Will resorted to leaning forward in his stool staring down at the bar with his hand over his bald head muttering and laughing to himself. The three girls at the end would clearly be of no help and the working class two would not even look up when I spoke to them so I headed over to the three booths on the other end of the bar.

The booth in the far corner across from the busted jukebox was occupied by one lone man passed out in front of a full glass of beer identical to everyone else's. I could smell the piss rising off him so I gave him a pass. The two other booths were filled. To the left were two couples sitting across from each other. They were two young guys in baseball caps and jerseys with two cute girls who seemed to laugh anytime either one of them said anything. They were talking loudly and drinking hard. I walked up to the table. Placed my hands down on it and leaned in to the kid on my left.

"Excuse me. Just what the hell is going on here?" The young man looked at me, shook his head slightly with widened eyes and turned his attention to the conversation. The boy on the other side blurted "Just try to enjoy yourself, man." and launched into an over exaggerated account of a priest and a rabbi that there was no possible chance that anyone over the age of twelve in the country had not heard before. None the less the laughter rang from their mouths. "Dipshit college kids," I muttered and turned away which brought about more laughs from their inebriated faces.

I turned to the last table. It was empty besides an old man. He was hunched over his beer. His remaining hair was white, his skin clung to his bones and he smiled as I turned to him. He held a burning cigarette in his hand that he was tapping into a nearly full ashtray. There were three more full ashtrays jammed with butts next to it and five more empty ones were stacked off to the side. He held a bony veined hand out to me. I shook it gladly and said "Hey I was wondering if you could help me?" He nodded slightly reached into his pocket and pulled out a small device that he pressed to his throat. It began to hum loudly and for a moment I could make out what he said although it sounded as if a voice was being pushed through a the blades of a fan. "I'd be happy to" he hummed, "the…" the little device quit running for a moment. He grimaced, banged the device against the table until it began to vibrate once again placed it to his throat and emitted "the key is to drink more." His little portable voice box quit again. He banged it against the table twice more but it refused to spring back to life. He placed it back in his pocket, turned to me with a smile, cocked his head, shrugged, placed another butt in the ashtray and drank deeply of his beer before digging another cigarette from the pack.

"Am I the only one in this place that is not totally fucked!" I yelled looking around the bar for anyone with any sense.

"No," yelled one of the frat boys "You're totally fucked too!"

"Alright that's it!"

I had no idea how I arrived here. I had only slightly more of a concept of why everyone in this hole seemed to be a tad more insane than the worst patron of any bar I had ever spent any time in, but I was leaving.

I jumped on the empty seat of the booth across from the piss smelling man and began to feel along the wall. The walls were painted plain white and were seamless as far as I could tell but there must be a doorway concealed somewhere and I needed to find it. I needed to get the hell out of here.

I balled my fingers into a fist and tapped the wall. I was hoping to hear a hollow knock and fully prepared to hear the sound of percussion that nearly anyone can tell you means you have rapped your fist upon a solid wall, but I was not prepared for the result my rapping achieved.

When I knocked upon the wall I heard nothing.

There was no reverberation at all. I met a solid surface. I felt it. I placed my palm in disbelief upon it, but when I knocked upon the wall there was no sound. I had never experienced such a thing. No one on the planet with hearing has. Then again, perhaps I was standing on a ripped green upholstered booth that did not exist in the plane I was accustomed to but when I rang my knuckles upon this wall there was no sound.

Hesitantly, I drew back my fist and punched the wall with a soft glancing blow. There was no thud of impact though the nerves in my hand let me know I hit something without give. I suppressed the urge to begin pounding on the wall, momentarily laughed out of disbelief and, awash in absurdity, looked around to see if there was anyone else in the bar that thought these circumstances were at all strange.

No. There I was standing on a booth laughing out loud to myself and knocking on the wall in disbelief and no one even seemed to notice.

I leaned down, swooped up the full beer sitting in front of the unconscious man, who smelled worse than the last hobo I'd given a dollar to, poured the worst drink I had ever had down my open throat, resisted the urge to smash the glass upon the back of the head of the frat boy in the booth beside me and bellowed "I don't know what the fuck is going on here, but I'm leaving. This bar is shit."

I hopped down from the booth and headed back to the bar. Frat boy #1 commented to the rest of his table as I passed. It was some remark about fresh fish and of course they all thought it was hilarious.

The only person in the whole place that had done more than momentarily look up from their drinks as I walked with purpose back to the bar following my declaration was Will.

"Hey I know that look, don't do anything stupid," Will said as I walked back to the bar. "Trust me, there's no need to get the management," he continued as I walked past him, "C'mon man let me buy you a drink," he said louder as I took the bar stool in both hands and lifted it over my head followed by "Shit man, don't say I didn't warn you" I spun around and took a running swing with the barstool into the wall where I had mysteriously arrived.

There was no thud as the metal stool slammed into the wall. The full overhead swing failed to leave a mark but the vibrations that rang down the legs of the stool carried through me. It felt as if it loosened my teeth. My whole body rang with the blow and I dropped the stool upon the ground.

"Do we have a problem here?"

I looked up and Dave had materialized behind the bar. "Why don't you have a seat?" He calmly said and surely enough the barstool I had just slammed into the wall and dropped to the floor had returned to its place right next to Big Will. I glanced back down and saw empty space where my seat had just been.

"Somebody better tell me what is going on here." I demanded.

"Look," Dave said "We try to be patient with new comers but if you continue to cause trouble I'll have to get my boss." No one seemed aware of what was happening. They all continued talking or drinking except Will who merely swallowed hard, shook his head and said "No. Don't do this man."

I knew the fear of a cornered animal then. I knew the desperation in the last ineffectual snap of a wolf's jaws before being euthanized. I knew the futile rage an animal in captivity knows as it throws itself against the bars.

There was something inside me I had held back for a very long time. Something I had perhaps suppressed my entire life. Something rose from within me and curled my hands into white knuckled, shaking fists. Wherever I had kept this part of myself for as long as I had existed could no longer hold it and rage turned my vision red. My teeth clenched so tightly they hurt and I was left with no alternative. I was going to kill Dave.

I walked around to the end of the bar and in my head I could see just how the bartender would look with both of my hands wrapped around his throat. I could see how his eyes would bulge as he choked to death. I could see how satisfying it would be to kill this man.

"I would love to meet the management," I said coldly "And explain to him why I did what I am about to do to you."

As I walked purposefully around the bar Dave simply responded "You know customers are not allowed behind the bar." And as I stepped behind the bar, as I placed my foot from the thin grey carpeting that covered the floor to the linoleum laid upon the floor behind the bar I found myself in the manager's office.

I was standing in the office of a typical restaurant except, once again, there were no doors. There was a desk covered in papers. An outdated monitor and keyboard sat at its edge. There were two chairs one sitting facing the desk and one behind it. Leaning back in the seat behind the desk sat a pudgy middle aged man with glasses, black hair, stubble, yellow teeth, and a slightly upturned nose. The walls were covered in framed photos of varying sizes with two large pictures dominating the wall behind the man who wore a gold name tag pinned to his striped white shirt with the word "Management" stamped upon it.

He looked up briefly from a conversation he was having on the phone.

I was suddenly quite calm. He looked up from his call, held his hand over the receiver and said "Give me one minute would you? I have to take this. Have a seat."

I did exactly as he said and sat. The call did not take long. The feeling that came over me when I entered the room was one of complete obedience. I took a look at the two pictures over his head as I waited.

There were two framed photographs. They were both of him with his arm around someone standing in front of the purple neon Liver Failure sign hanging over the bar. The one on the left was undeniably him posing with John Belushi. The one on the right was him shaking hands with the former president Bill Clinton.

"Okay, John," the management said "Okay, so he'll get the axe, look I have to go I have an unsatisfied customer. Right. Right. Bye." He hung the phone and smiled. "I see you recognize the two of them. Yeah John Belushi was with us for quite some time great guy, and former president Clinton always loves to visit. Chris, let me ask you something. If I were to very slowly lower you into boiling oil would you like to be lowered head first or feet first?"

"Feet first"

"That's what I said too. Chris you have a lot of potential. I like you I do. So I'm going to take it easy on you. This is your first offense and a lot of people tend to get a little upset when they first arrive. You may be here a very long time and we'd like to keep you on so I'm gonna have to ask that you behave more professionally with the staff. Try to relax. Have yourself a drink and enjoy yourself okay. Cigar?"

There was no emotion in me. I was empty, open to his every suggestion; my actions were contingent on his every word. He asked if I wanted a cigar and I responded with the answer.

"No thanks, I don't smoke."

"Okay." He leaned back in his chair opened a desk drawer and took out a large cigar and a cutter. "A transition like this can be hard I know, okay, but I need you to take this meeting seriously so I'm gonna have to ask you to stand."

I stood and waited for him to tell me what to do next.

He took the cigar, inserted it into the circular hole of the cutter and said "Now I want you to look straight ahead for a moment. Just relax and watch what I'm about to do." The management then clipped the tip of the cigar off.

I felt something hit my shoe as the tip of the cigar fell to the floor. It also felt as if I pissed myself. I could feel my groin grow wet and warm. I could feel fluid run down the insides of my legs. No thought passed through my mind as to what just happened. I was told to look straight ahead and relax and that is what I did.

The management paused for a moment to light his cigar as more hot fluid ran from my crotch down my legs.

"Now" he said "I want you to look down and I want you to think about what has just happened. I don't want you to say anything or make any other movement than to look down okay? Just remain calm and take a look."

I looked down.

There was a large red patch of blood bleeding through my pants and spreading down the front of my legs. My penis had apparently been cut from my body, had fallen down my left pant leg, and was resting on the top of my left shoe.

"Okay now I'm gonna send you back out to the bar okay but to avoid any problems like this in the future I'm gonna let you feel what I've done to you for just a moment. I want you to know that we value you as a customer and that this is merely a warning. So please be nice to Dave and I don't want to see you in my office again."

How does one describe pain? There are words we've invented to match sensations like pain. Agony would be a fitting one for this situation I suppose. In the moment it took me to close my eyes I was in more agony than I had ever been in my entire existence and in the next moment, in the time it takes to blink, I found myself coming to at the bar face down with my arm as a pillow and a lukewarm glass of beer before me.

I stood up quickly, knocking the stool out from beneath me, gasping for air and pulled my zipper down to get a good look at what was left of my dick.

Everything was right where it was supposed to be.

Big Will glanced over at me with my dick out and said "Jesus, man, he went for your dick. You must be a preferred customer." To my right the beautiful mute just giggled and when the tramp stamp two noticed, they began another round of scowling and bitching. "Hey little guy why don't you tell your owner to put you away before you make me get sick all over the bar!" yelled the ugly one closest to me while the woman sitting further down just yelled "Put your dick back in your pants!"

"Just because this is the closest you'll ever get to one is no reason to get all upset ya pair of fuckin' cows!" Big Will bellowed back his face turning red "I've never choked a stupid bitch in each hand but I've always wanted to!" He then leaned to me and said "I swear those girls were placed here solely to make our lives a living hell. The middle one's name may as well be Temptation and the two bitches at her side are her hell hound guard dogs."

No one else in the bar even looked up. The girls went back to talking about whatever it was they always seemed to be talking about and Will went back to his drink. I put my dick back in my pants, picked up the barstool and sat back down. I needed a drink and fortunately in this place there was always a drink. There was always one more drink and very little else. I picked up the beer before me and poured some of it down my throat. I didn't mind that it was warm and cheap. It arrested some deep tremor within me so I finished it.

I suppose I reacted in the same way so many do when faced with something so utterly improbable. I reacted the same way one would when in line at a pharmacy and the woman in front of you is wearing only a bra for a top. I reacted the same way one would when a homeless man walks past yelling incoherently at whatever it is in his head that is trying to convince him to burn a local library to the ground. When faced with something that rallies against everything you have constructed in your mind to be your everyday reality, we all do the same thing. We react casually. We go on as if nothing was out of the ordinary. To act in any other way would acknowledge that what we have fought to identify as our lives is an illusion. My response was an offhanded comment.

"This is the weirdest thing that has ever happened to me in my entire life," I said to Will as I clasped and unclasped my penis through my jeans with one hand.

"No it's not." Will said "Your life ended the moment you arrived. You seem like a nice enough guy. How did you wind up here?"

"Actually I'm not sure. I guess I'm no more of an asshole than most. What about you, Will?"

"That's a good question…"

It was then that Will began to tell me of nearly everything he had ever done wrong. It was as if there was a deep reservoir of guilt that had dammed up within Big Will his entire life and my one innocuous inquiry had placed a payload of dynamite at the base of what held his remorse.

For what must have been hours, Will talked of his life. He spoke of every intentional misdeed. I became very uncomfortable the moment he began and pounded back beer after beer. I listened intently for his sake, however, as I felt it was of great importance to bear witness to Will's sins. My only response was to nod between drinks and occasionally mutter "Jesus, Will…" to emphasize that he still held my attention.

He began with tales of shoplifting and pushing his sister down the stairs and then went on to bullying others and cheating in school. He then told me of the priest at his local church that had molested him as a boy and how this had driven him to renounce god. He told me of illegitimate children he had refused to care for in any way, and how he'd turned his back on his own mother when she grew ill and had turned to him to care for her. He was thorough. He even went so far as to confess to me every year in which he'd cheated on his taxes or how once he'd scratched a car parking his own and driven off after checking to see that no one was looking.

As he told me every faulty deed he could recall, I drank. I drank until the world around me grew fuzzy at the edges and my responses slowed and Big Will finally finished his confession.

"…and I suppose that's how I came to be a long time patron of the Liver Failure." he said.

"Jesus, Will." I said to him one last time. I looked down at my nearly empty drink trying to think of a proper response. Something to make my new pal feel better about what he just told me. Something to make all of what had happened to the both of us up to this point in our lives okay or just a little brighter for a moment, at least. It occurred to me that Big Will had gotten a raw deal. It didn't seem to me that a guy like him ever stood a chance at not winding up in a place like this. He'd clearly had it hard. He'd lost his place in the world from a young age and had no one around worthy or willing to put him back on track. Yeah he'd fucked up. We all fuck up. Yeah he did a lot of things he regretted. We all do. Whoever or whatever had the power to place us into our lives to test us would also have preordained our every failure. That Will had been placed hip deep in shit and then been asked to wade through it smelling of roses. Fuck that. All of this occurred to me in a drunken haze as I looked down into my glass, so I emptied it and turned to Will to tell him.

Will's stool was empty. I turned to look for him and there he was standing behind the bar. "Can I get you another?" Will asked.

"Will, what the hell are you doin' behind the bar?'

"I've been promoted." He said, fingering his name tag. "One more?"

"Will what the hell you mean you've been promoted? How…?"

"Better to reign in hell than to serve in heaven." Will said proudly "By the way management wants to see you."

The tremors began then and I knew them for what they were. My heart spasmed, the movement surged into my chest and down my arms leaving my clenched fists shaking once again. Just before the shudders claimed my mind I had a flash of realization as to their origin. I had felt a rippling such as this before but never with so much intensity, never with so much strength, never had it grasped me so closely.

This was the urge. This was the temptation embodied. This was the evil impulse behind every misdeed with never before seen strength and this took hold of me in a violent rage.

I leaned over the bar and grabbed Will by the scruff and yanked him clean over the bar, pulling as I stepped back until he slid over and fell face first, hands outstretched in an attempt to cushion his fall, to the floor at my feet.

As Big Will whimpered my name I began to kick him, every blow aimed at his face.

"Fuck you, Big Will!" I shouted. My first kick grazed his ear and landed on his shoulder.

"You're an asshole." I said as my foot connected with his forehead.

"Your mother needed you! Your children needed you!" Big Will cried out and curled into a ball, covering his face with his hands and in response I began to stomp on his exposed head.

"There's no excuse! What the priest did to you is no excuse!" I brought my foot down on his temple, hard.

"You want to serve in hell, well I'll give you hell." I stepped to the side and kicked him in his undefended stomach. "You're a piece of shit, Big Will. I could forgive you for everything you've done in life!"

He lowered his guard to avoid another kick to the gut and I planted my foot into his teeth reddening the tip of my shoe. "Spit out your teeth and get me a beer, bartender." I said loud and cold as I reached to the bar for the waiting filled glass and threw it at his head although it only bounced off his elbow.

"I'm gonna smash this glass in your face and slit your throat with it." I reached back to the bar where, surely enough, another glass awaited. I picked it up off the bar and leaned over Big Will, then got in close and I raised my arm, ready to smash the glass into his skull.

A five fingered steel clamp took my arm and I went limp. I looked up, using all my strength to lift my head as I was pulled from my feet and saw what was and was not Dave. His dimensions seemed to fill the room. His proportions were larger than could physically fit into the space in which he stood. His eyes were glowing coals. His expression gave more meaning to the word grim than can be expressed in words. I dangled in his grasp and he shook my limp form with every syllable he spoke. I seemed to hang miles from a carpeted floor that was just below me and he seemed to loom impossibly high above me though he held me close to his face.

"I think you've had enough" he said, breathing heat into my face. He flicked me then with the ease one takes waiving smoke from one's face over the bar. I cracked my head hard against the wall soundlessly and fell to the floor, an unconscious heap.

There I was, standing in that same little cramped office with the management sitting behind his desk. His hands were folded, his elbows propped up and he looked very concerned. Unlike the first time I had been taken to see the management I did not feel calm. I felt as if, for some reason, this time I would be lucky to leave with only a dose of severe pain.

"How are you feeling, Chris?" he asked and without waiting for a response went on. "Now I realize that visits to my office can be nerve wracking and so most of the time I do my best to make a customer feel calm, but I'm going to go ahead and leave how you feel about this visit entirely up to you. Have a seat."

I sat down, leaning slightly forward in my chair trying not to focus on the spattering of blood on my shoe or the sweat running down my face. I was very much afraid that he would offer me a cigar. I was very much afraid I had nearly killed Big Will. I was very much afraid.

"Okay now, do you remember the girl you dated in high school? You know the one you talked into having an abortion?" asked the Management.

I was stunned that he made no mention of the beating. "Yeah I was really young and..."

"Let me finish. Management doesn't really look very highly on that sort of thing. I've been looking over your file and it seems that that was the deciding factor in making you a patron of my establishment but after looking into your records more deeply I've discovered that had this boy Nick been born, that would have been your son's name by the way, he would have gone on, through very little fault of either of you or his mother, to be involved in a very violent school shooting so I've discussed it with the rest of the staff and I'm gonna go on ahead and put you in for a transfer. Okay, we loved having you and you're welcome to come back anytime."

As the last words fell from his mouth everything went black. I was falling and spinning clockwise through nothing and yet my hands clenched something soft on either side of me. I spun and slipped away for what seemed like a very long time. Finally, everything slowed and stopped and a bright light pierced my eyes and I found myself lying in a hospital bed staring up at fluorescent lighting a thin blanket clutched in each hand at my sides. My head throbbed so badly I wanted it removed and my mouth had never been so dry.

I was in the hospital for several days recovering from a self induced case of alcohol poisoning. I didn't talk much of my experience except in Alcoholics

Anonymous and they all thought that I was crazy and therefore I fit right in. I wish I could say that I never had another drink after that, but I fight hard every day with varying levels of success.

I did call the mother of my unborn son Nick though. I was horrified that she would tell me how much she hated me or that I would make the mistake of telling my story to her, but she's doing fine. We agreed to meet for coffee sometime but most likely never will.

I do my best not to convince myself that it was all a hallucination and to ensure I never return to that bar.

I suppose I'm lucky. A lot of people hit bottom. I guess my bottom wasn't really that far down. I suppose I fell softly enough.

I think of that dive bar often when I consider walking down to the one on my corner. At times these thoughts alone are enough to drive me to the establishment's doors. I think of the beating I gave a friend, of the irresistible urge that led me to do such a thing and how it still leads me in every decision I make. I think of Big Will serving drinks for an eternity with busted teeth only to be promoted to sitting in that tiny office torturing others and snapping photos with random celebrities, living or dead. I think of the other patrons and their solution to the existence they had found themselves in.

I think I can avoid going back. Perhaps I cannot avoid placing another drink to my lips, acting in anger, or committing another sin. I may have learned a lesson that I cannot apply, but I think of my time spent at the Liver Failure. How it has changed what life I have left and how easily a return trip can be arranged. There will always be a stool for the willing, a stool at that bar for so many of us, a stool at that bar for me. I had earned my place in that seat and now I must be worthy of never returning to it.

Breakfast

Carefully cracked open upon the world

I lie in the yolk of my mind curled

from warmth, to shell

to griddle, to plate

from the first word spoken

to the last meal ate

from a change in perception

to an altered mental state

melancholy, fat and jolly

anorexic, sick

mind numbing

the things

that make us humans tick

Nick Liu grabbing me by the collar as I fell

Danny Wiedner with a gun to my face

with a "give me my fucking money motherfucker"

The view of Houston from a life flight helicopter

that last grasp for rock looking down at a long fall

the scream in every single last man's mind when they nearly miss

that fatal accident

that left turn on a busy street

the squeal of those brakes

We talk to our pets and no one minds yet speaking to yourself in public is enough to clear seats on the bus,

some keep the overcooked remains of loved ones on their mantles yet refuse to speak to those relatives that have grown distant through disagreement or a gap in geography or merely a matter of time since they last contacted them, blood forms a bond to some that is stronger than the realization that they would rather never see an individual ever again,

the misled children of many have strained themselves over the naked countenances of brothers sisters and cousins in an effort to keep their blood clean, keep their skin pale or their hair blonde, to keep the color of one's eyes just right, to keep the name after their first that at times hold so much sway, nobility, or property, it is ironic that this practice only led to defective bodies and minds that the introduction of fresh flesh would have easily remedied,

we often times forget that we all originate, are composed of, and live for the flesh, that after a varying amount of decades we are only what we have created through a varying amount of contact with the flesh of others, though life does not require a genetic slug that would remain from firing ones shell to be remembered. To leave one's mark behind in the souls of those you've brushed against through time is not traditionally considered family though I consider that unfortunate,

as a child a blood brother, to press one's bloody wound

to that of a friend, was considered a privilege when in this time it merely brings to mind the horror of a disease consisting of capital letters and the use of a condom,

to age in interest of one's own sex must be difficult as I know my traditional interests at a young age were, as boys we all knew what we were required to desire before we were aware of what the end result would even become, we sat side by side envious of the lying older boys and the sons of fathers that still resided at home and hid their adult literature poorly, in middle school we discussed within tight circles after the pretense was turned out with the lights where the vagina could be found and where the easy girls' lockers existed, to this day I consider myself fortunate to have had the companions of my age around to clear my mind of the doubt that I was clearly alone on the earth with nothing but my curiosity and the occasional frontal nudity found on the television past midnight, I fail to conceive of the method of the kids of the new age, one needs merely an internet connection a personal computer and a lack of parental control to access material I have no knowledge of or would rather not know, the mere description of "two girls one cup" was sufficient to bring my friends to retching,

the consistence with which the male of the species brings sex to mind can be disturbing to some, and the consistence of which women consider such things can be quite intriguing, after reflection I'd say that with men the occurrence seems excessive yet as a man I'd add that as far as women are concerned it occurs far too infrequently regardless of the amount that it occurs, I have and do consider that the greatest result of aging as a man is that I fail to contemplate sex at every turn and now think of it only three turns out of four,

Within me is a madman

His rotted yellow teeth are always in view. He screams,
laughs, and cries out or just stands, mouth agape,
breathing in my ear,

He is not always within me. At times he wears my skin.
At times he claims everything I think myself to be.

I am not always aware of his location, be it tucked
deep, curled up in the corner mumbling quietly, or
within my mind, his filthy hands wrapped around my
throat forming every word I emit.

At times I care for him. I take a moment to feed him. I
take an hour to clean the filth from beneath his nails, to
wipe the dirt from a face whose only clean patches are
where the tears have ran.

I would spend more time with this madman. I would
welcome his presence in me and care more for him than
I would myself. I would love him as a parent. I would
tend to him as a good son cares for his elderly mother.

I am afraid of this madman though I love him. I am
afraid to welcome him into the home that is me in fear
that I will awake one morning and some of the things
which I possess will be missing, or, worse yet, it will no
longer be my home at all and I will be the guest to be
evicted at the madman's whim.

I am afraid I will be within the madman rather than the

madman within me.

So something within me is unwelcome.

It would be more humane to euthanize him but I cannot.
It would be more humane to return him to the wild, but
I have claimed his habitat.

I fear this madman, but he is too crazed to fear me in
return.

Within me I build a cage for a madman. He escapes,
repairs to his cell are made, and he is thrown back in
when I have him in my grasp.

The place I make for him never holds him, so please

Within me is a madman. Have you seen him?

Crusade

Tiring of the presence of taint in the nectar of my soul.

Climbing the walls, and ceilings, until I can no longer tell which is which.

Armor plated in snug fitting angst.

I've sought god

from Allah

to Jerusalem,

and found him in you.

Every one of you

that has heard

these words in themselves.

Eloquence dribbled from my mouth and stained

my clothing

the earth

the air

the others

mouths hung agape

I said many, many things

none of which I felt mattered

none of which should have mattered

the idea that predesignated combinations of noises have
the power to

insult

alter

injure

heal

does not sit well in my mind

at least,

that's one way to put it.

Crissy

I was immediately attracted to her

      We talked for a while, several hours

      We both lived with our parents

      Neither of us had a job

She seemed interested

When I left the bar she called me sweetheart

I found myself going to the pub with my father on
Wednesdays hoping to see her again

      We met several times

The last time I saw her she didn't remember my name

One night she was talking to my dad

When she leaned in and kissed him

I finished my beer and left

I don't think of her anymore

And pretend I'm not disappointed.

To yawn before the hungry lion

To rip the eye of the shark upon bleeding into the waves

To request the jagged rings of your opponent stay on

Those with the instinct drag themselves, broken limbed, from the wild and its elements

Some need the hardship of the frugal

Some need the pain of isolation

Some survive the incredibly treacherous

While others are slain by their own hand upon reclining chairs

facing the glow of the television, and the poison of the diet of those who do not lack

drink the spirits only to face the challenge of steadying oneself

imbibe of the smoke to challenge the lung

it takes me less to die than family and friends

consume all you can now

that you may draw upon food's storage when the

stomach shrinks and the mouth loses a task

draw blood from the fingertip as you lack the ink and
paint

the vow merely words until action meets them with
sincerity

early man's knuckles dragged upon the ground that they
may pluck the fruit without having to climb the tree

many deny the emotions clearly viewed in the eye of
the beast

better that than to accept that you may share traits with
a monster

Truth

The truth is venomous.

Lies feel good,

and sometimes,

venom can cure you

Bravery

I saw a blind man walking down the sidewalk.

No dog, no friend, just walking alone, tap, tap, tapping with his cane.

Strutting through darkness led only by the touch of a stick in his hand, and the sound of the street around us I take for granted.

He walked with more confidence, more certainty, than I ever have.

I saw him and thought, "That is the bravest man I have ever seen."

Bargaining

There are at least five stages of grief

The fanged beast that rears its ugly head and gnaws at
my flesh is the stage known as bargaining

It involves focusing on what you could've done
differently

If I had been there to remind her to check her insulin

If I had cared for her enough to restrict her diet, to
make her last years more fulfilled, to heal her in ways I
had not conceived of and cannot do

Had I not let her live on her own after years of caring
for her

Had I not let her make her own choices

Had I not failed

Had there been no mistakes

Had I been there

Had I had the foresight even Nostradamus lacked and
the sheer will, the mental prowess, to cure her

Had I had the diplomacy to push stem cell research to

its fullest potential and our healthcare beyond its current boundaries

Had I found the cure among test tubes and lab results I do not understand

She was my mother, Trudie Hochhalter, she was my closest friend, and she was a source of guidance and inspiration

The stage known as bargaining tells me it was my actions that led her to die

While the level of enlightenment I have achieved tells me that death is a force that has existed as long as life

Still the morning of December 7th 2012 held a sunrise I will never forget

And there will be a day among all of the fortunate that we will leave such a date etched in those we've loved

There will be other sunrises I will never forget

There will also be other sunrises that spare me of grief and regret

There is no bargaining with a sunrise

It is best

It is the best thing to think that purity stinks, and all that
is evil is not ugly

It is the best thing to know, that life is a show, and it's
best that your costume fits snugly

It is best not to ask for the unspoken task, for what's out
of sight is out of mind

It is best not to quote all the things I've wrote, best to
leave these dead thoughts behind

It is best to know, the ejaculatory flow will mostly end
sans disappointment

It is best to accept the fact, that you're lacking in tact
and god rubs out life like an ointment

It is best not to guess, who you need to impress, to treat
all life as one and the same

And finally I say, all life's color is gray, and we all play
along with the game

Lacking the Nerve to Look My Reflection in the Eyes

The burden proves light on my shoulders,

yet blankets my mind in uncertainty.

Unsure if those at my door are guests,

I invite them all in.

Invite them to wallow in my hospitality.

Define my sense of self.

Rub shoulders with society

as I see it.

Never seeming to dictate the time when

they should leave.

Grasping for an acceptance from others that

I already possess.

Internally I am inevitably alone,

unacceptable in my own regard.

I go on with a white-knuckled grip,

holding nothing in my clenched fists.

Seeking release,

failure is a preference,

to choking eternally on my anticipations.

My First Pet

It was as good as dead when I found it lying in a driveway.

A car had crushed the rear half of its body but the poor little lizard still lived.

I suppose if I'd come across it today I'd keep walking, or finish the job.

That would have been the merciful thing to do.

I'd never had my own pet and, for some reason, I thought I could save it.

I scraped it off the pavement, put it in a bucket full of grass, and took it to school.

We had a few lizards for pets in my class, and I thought he would fit right in.

When I gave the bucket to my teacher she didn't say much.

She just took the bucket and said she would see what she could do.

She told me several hours later that my lizard was dead.

I cried as only a child cries.

My Twenty First

I had four or five drinks in front of me.

I came to the bar with a couple of friends. Not close friends but close enough to want to take me out on the twenty first on a weekday to get drunk

I approached the bar with I.D. in hand and asked for a free drink.

"Yeah, I'll give you a shot. Ever had a cement mixer?"

Never have a cement mixer.

A cement mixer is two shots one shot of clear liquor and one shot of cream.

You take a shot of cream; hold it in your mouth and follow with the liquor.

When the liquor hit the cream it curdled in my mouth.

I chewed the first drink down.

I had planned on tipping the bartender.

It was a Thursday night and all my friends wanted was to get me shitfaced and go home.

I'd had six drinks with a couple more in front of me when they decided we'll all play a game of darts.

I kept drinking.

I drank enough to start shutting down. I didn't laugh or talk, I just stared off into space.

I won the game of darts.

It was a complete fluke.
I just did my best to keep my darts on the board, and I won the damn game.

"It's not affecting him," one of them said and more drinks arrived.

I followed my friend Sam and his girl Christine back to their place. They put me up on the couch in their living room.

I made many trips to the bathroom and the drinks tasted worse going up than going down.

I was lying on the couch and listening to the sound of my friends fuck when their door opened.

"Do it. Do it. Just ask him."

My friend Sam's head peaked around the corner

"Do you want in on this?" he asked.

I waved him off and limped my way back to the bathroom to dry heave.

It cannot be said I will ever forget what I can remember of my twenty first birthday.

The center of the top of my head is the point at which trouble splits.

As a wood splitter does the two ends of what I am dealing with lands in each hand outstretched.

I must hold the two halves of the log for a time whether I choose to or not.

However, they keep coming and I must hold each half in each hand for a time to judge their weight.

I have no choice how quickly the cut ends of torment are split. I have no choice of how many, nor their weight, nor their length.

At times the split ends of stress spill from my hands and fall to the pool of anguish below. However they are still mine to carry. However they are still mine to lift to the pile I stack to the side and pray I will never need to burn on a cold lonely night.

At times the splitter needs no use. The point that splits them gains rest as well as the arms that hold them, as well as the same arms that haul them to the side, split trouble after split ordeal.

There will come a time when the point in my head is too dull to split, when the arms that bear the burden that is wrought will be too weak to lift a single branch of sorrow.

At this point I am quite sure that there will be no one

with the strength, the will, to lift or split for me.

And so there is another heavy log in the splitter.

And so there is my life.

Average

No one ever hears the

Tales of the less than beautiful

Tales of the less than ugly

Tales of those who reach their goal unremarkably
without the thunder of applause or the bright white
flashes of light

Tales of those who fail in less than a grandiose way
without the courtroom battle or news coverage

Those who form merely a passing face

On the lifelong feature film that is existence

Those who exist

Exist

As merely a dot

On the inkblot

Of what our minds perceive

The semi-successful

Working nine to five

One hundred and sixty hours a month

Answering the questions of the

Boss, co-worker, employee, employer,

Answering the phones that ring without mercy

Answering the questions that define monotony

Within every being there exists a screaming of desperation

A voice that demands one is defined

Individually and universally

As unique

To define oneself in words that no one can

In words that ring true to the

Claws that grasp the flesh of life

to pull oneself upward to the light of

life and death

being universally sought and universally found

finding desperation within

and holding complacency before oneself as a candle in the night as the wax drips

so our existence rises from within and drips from our
exterior

burning those who grasp it

pooling below to form

something new

It's not enough and it is

It's enough that my car does not always start,

that I am one check from a life in the street,

that my mother's ashes sit on my sister's mantle for less than three weeks.

I am filled to the brim with my job, a roommate who will not leave though I will no longer accept his rent. My cup overflows with the endless trials that, once overcome, leave no reward, and are followed too closely by another.

I cannot wait until the day I die. I cannot wait until I have a day of peace. In this way I have had plenty. In these ways I have had enough.

It is not enough that my bed remains empty when I wake.

It is not enough that I wish to be alone at times while longing for someone to talk to.

It is not enough that I still rely on my father to pay some of my bills.

The glass at my bedside lacks enough water to wet my dry mouth in the middle of the night.

I lack the education to solve the equation I face every day.

The tube that held the ointment that stops the aching for a time has been squeezed empty.

There are not enough pills on my dresser to assuage me. There is no amount of words traded with any being on this planet to put my mind to rest.

How is it that one side of the scale lacks even a layer of dust while the other holds an improbable amount? At one time, I am sure, there was balance, and I tell myself that there will be again.

But that is not enough though I have no choice but for it to be.

I still breathe.

I still fill my mouth and chew.

I press the keys on the outdated machine that indicates I have shown up on time whenever I am required.

I ask the questions that allow others to continue to speak to me and push the air through my vocal chords in the proper way to make them laugh or smile.

I lift one foot at a time, move it forward, set it down and then again with the other.

All things considered that is enough.

Existence

They are not all heard

Some pass by you like a whisper

Others rake themselves across your

body

face

 soul

They all claw their way

in

to the ground as their feet sink in earth

in

to the sky as their heads rise and fall with each step

in to each other's lives to sit dumbly or glow with
brilliance

desperate to alter

to leave something behind

to show that they have been

Addicted

I know that I am addicted when I desire another smoke
or another beer

Even though I am holding both in my hands

I've seen

I've seen a cat swung by its tail until it flew away, tail still in the boys hand

I've seen my life flash before my eyes

More than once

I've seen the world melt around me

The acid helped

I've seen myself lying on a stretcher from twenty feet up, surrounded by ambulances

I thought "that guy could stand to lose some weight"

I've seen my cousin, lifeless, at the bottom of a pool

I've seen monks defy the laws of physics

I've seen planes smash into skyscrapers

I've seen the moon eclipse the sun

The healthy crawl while the legless run

I've seen an ear bitten off in a fight

A great, all knowing, immense ball of light

Webbed toes and extra appendages

Sufferers of stigmata wrapped in bandages

I've seen hundreds applaud my acting

Bodies stacked high like tinder

A great man bring peace by not eating

A blazing inferno wrought by just a single cinder

I've seen fire created from ice

My own head covered in lice

I've drank God's blood and eaten God's flesh

I've seen people feed milk to their deity

The rise and collapse of society

The poor tip the rich

The infertile give birth

The morbidly obese with a thousand pound girth

Genetically engineered glow in the dark monkeys

I've seen women wed women

And men loving men

I've saved a man's life

And I'd do it again

I've seen the millennia pass

Kurt Kobain dead

History's best grass

Snakes with extra heads

I've seen blind men paint well

Computer driven mice

The burning gates of hell

Nearly died twice

I've seen Bruce Lee give beatings

Ali take a punch to the teeth

Limbed fish breathing air

Tectonic plates grinding beneath

I've seen sixty pound tumors removed

A baby given a new heart

Music that touched me so deeply

I wouldn't know where to start

All these things that I've seen, that I've felt, that I've learned

All fall to this page, and the unspoken word

I have not known the sensation of firing when I've seen the whites of their eyes or hearing the grunt of a man's last breath leaving his body, of leaning over the corpse of a comrade as he loses the feeling in his soon to be cold carapace, of the final shudder, of the view of an onslaught of bullet or bayonet or the cracking of limbs or the crushing of a ribcage,

I have never grown accustomed to the weight of a Kevlar helmet or the Velcro straps of a vest tightly gripping one's thorax, pleading they shoot me where it holds, may they shoot me where this holds,

many are grateful that the doctor's kit no longer consists of merely bandages and saw, that now they may often save the limb and the entirety of which is attached, the old ways held honor in that they faced one another with line upon line of human soldier ants, that they would take their turns to attack and allow the women to drag the bodies from the field before they volleyed again,

this approach may have seemed noble to some at the time that those firing from cover or sending the messenger back sans head was ungentlemanly like, but this is a lie, as one may say taking the king in chess in a matter of moves would be considered low, there is truth in the unlimited violence, at times taking the field without honor honors the men that were spared, the game lacks honor but for the honor of the victor,

when aircraft first began to be used in battle they

considered retreating from its over head passage to be cowardly and instead insisted the men upon which the machine bore down turn, hold ground, and fire upon it as it strafed the brave children of earth, it is to be noted that this practice did not last long and that not many know of this fault line of pride,

the inventor of the Gatling gun believed this invention would save many lives that the use of such a gun would reduce the quantity of men required to defend a given point, to say he was downtrodden with the effect of his invention would be a safe assumption

I enjoy the writer/director/producer element of the passing of time and the battles that lay like corpses strewn throughout the history of cinema, even within times of war, blood, and carnage, even those whose time may be partly spent entrenched in what our current form of combat has become, even those who subscribe, when left to their own devices, even those who partake of the media's form of battle of the handheld joystick and the crosshairs on the screen, of the dramatic close-up of the soldier who lies bleeding and shall soon pass, of the warfare of Hollywood and the playstation,

the martyrs of today lack the zeal of the warriors of old Valhalla, the vikings believed that when they fell upon the battlefield the beautiful winged valkyries would descend half naked with bodies and visages of only the most comely of women to snatch them from their suffering and bring them to a place where they could feast for all eternity, where every day they would charge into battle to cut and be cut to pieces only to be made whole for the next day's onslaught, the martyrs of today merely promise virgins or raisins and palaces within which they may enjoy them.

Soon the battles will only be close to home as all terrorism is and yet distant from the flesh of our soldiers, as distant as the man who guides the flight of a remote control unmanned aircraft armed to the teeth known aptly as the predator,

the gears, grinders, and meat slicers of war are oiled by the blood of its participants by the tears of the families in loss and fueled by the green fluid known as money, those who hold nothing dearest, nothing to their chest, are those that find peace.

Need

It can strike in a moment,

or fail to evolve over years

It smothers some,

Yet fails to inflict others

It carries you through life

And remains once you're gone

You carry it through life

and extinguish it when you leave

it's the reason for these words

what fueled you to read them

what has driven me to write them

the need to judge

the need to continue

or halt before the end

it is intangible

yet exists in every breath

every movement

every moment of consciousness

it creates and destroys us

We are undeniably in need

Parts of my life

The post office is an impossible excursion when you're
never conscious before six in the afternoon

The mail box imposing when all you receive is bills

A free e-mail account seems frivolous when all you
receive is spam

A doorbell merely noise when all welcome visitors
simply walk in

A cell phone goes unanswered when all calls are
marked as unknown

The rear passenger tire leaks but the gas station down
the street has free air as long as you hang up the hose

The overwhelming theme of Bukowski is what there
was to drink in any given prose

The cute girl you never had a chance with in high
school stopped chatting on facebook

Can't haul the Halloween decorations out of the garage
because of its proximity to the mattress filled with bed
bugs

The dusty exercise bike is the only thing standing
between me and a lifetime of obesity

Half a pack of smokes a day is as much taste of luxury as I need or can afford

I don't drink as much as I should yet more than I admit to my psychiatrist

My best friend has no idea why he deserves the title

The employees at the video store no longer ask my name

The headlights on my car don't seem to work in the snow or the rain

I have grown accustomed to driving in the dark

Awaiting rejections from the New Yorker becomes a welcome distraction

A friend says he needs shit that rhymes for his music and I'm happy to send it

The cable bill becomes an unavoidable expense

The student loans only cover one class at a time so I'll have my bachelor's degree at the age of thirty nine

Still dream about the pot though I am too psychotic to have smoked it in years

Ceased getting anxious about social interaction and now just get anxious about getting anxious

Am told they like my poetry but, the words, they mean nothing

Less than half of the eight spoken word CDs created
have ever been played

As a whole it seems meaningless but in its parts it
breaks down to nights with friends, evenings with my
brother, watching movies, and cleaning up the house

These parts make up my life

And if I could place them in my hands they would run
between my fingers

Sitting in the Restaurant of Life

I order the only thing on my menu,

"Shit sandwich, no mayo."

The coffee's not very good but the refills are relentless.

As I wait I glance around at the other tables.

Other people seem to be eating much better than I,

but no matter,

best to just focus on my plate.

The waitress arrives on cue with my meal.

Pretty much what I expected,

steaming flop,

two pieces of bread.

My server pauses to see if I'll actually eat it.

Afraid

Chills crawl up my neck like the fingers of a severed
hand

Hairs rise like bamboo bent from the air pushed
between the gaping maw of an immense terror

They say the tension is so thick it can be cut with a
knife but tension is the one that cuts

The beating of drums in my ears match the beats of my
heart

The fear sits beside me whispering to me and to repeat
what was said would be inhumane

To think you are strong enough to protect yourself from
fear, or fast enough to escape what you feel, is a form
of universal denial

Your muscles will lock leaving you unable to deliver a
single blow, you will twist an ankle fleeing and drag
yourself along far too slowly while the audience of your
subconscious screams at you to get your stupid ass up
and run

Every instance in which you have felt its whisper is a
cliché you've heard of many times yet every occurrence
of fright you've faced is a hard unwelcome kiss from a
stranger. Safety begs to be remembered.

Moments of Silence

I couldn't quite place it at first.

The streets seemed quieter than usual. The traffic thin, a few more cops about.

I walked into an empty bank.

The teller asked "Crazy what's going on isn't it?"

"What's that?" I asked.

There was a moment of silence, the first of many that day.

"The twin towers collapsed." she said.

"Really?" I walked away, lacking the impact of what had happened.

I didn't even know off the top of my head where the Twin Towers used to be.

When I got home I watched the news for twenty hours.

Listed Grievances

When I feel like it I pick my nose,

and yes,

occasionally I fart in public.

I have looked at your girlfriend's breasts,

if I've met her.

I am more likely to tell a friend to fuck off than a total
stranger.

I have disconnected myself from people I care about
with less notice than most people quit a job.

I have disrespected the emotions of my friends, my
family,

myself.

I am ashamed of myself,

ashamed enough for everyone in the room you are
standing in.

I knew you wouldn't like this poem when I wrote it,

but I wrote it anyway,

just to let you know,

that you're not alone.

Jeremy

I can't recall her name but she was my first real crush.

She was cute and was dating one of the popular kids.

We both wrote her poetry. She just ate that shit up.

She let him read my poetry and, in response, he began to cut himself.

I talked to him about it, while he held his slashed up hand, and he said he thought   my poetry was better.

It was.

I quit writing her poetry.

Spilt Milk

pools out before you

drips from the edge

which puddle to sop up

first

watching it drip from above

too high to reach

too late to stop

The meaning of things wrap themselves around you like a turban

the wording of things straighten the teeth

sounds drape themselves like long hairs across the ears

the feel of it calluses the palms

the length of it gives measure to each and every step

the breath gifts the tongue with a brutal eloquence

and the soul of it

belongs and is unique to every individual entity

Tap Tap Tap

Eight months ago my right hand started twitching.

It was nothing major. Every once in a while I noticed myself tapping my pointer finger against the tip of my thumb.

I'd seen my father with similar symptoms for years and encouraged him to see a neurologist but it took until yesterday to convince him.

Increasingly I find myself doing it, looking down at my hand as if it was someone else's.

This afternoon he told me my great grandfather died of Huntington's an incurable genetic neurological disorder that proved fatal for him at the age of forty four. I am thirty three.

I went to work an hour later and found myself too emotional to finish my shift.

I found myself asking my boss if I could leave early.

Asking him if he would tell those I work with why I was in tears so I would not have to.

As I write these words I find myself in sorrow.

In six days at around nine in the morning it will be two

months since my mother died.

As I write these words I think about saying something grand about hope, about faith, about an undeniable strength that others see in me even though it is rarely viewed in my own reflection.

But all I can think to say at this moment?

Is that I don't think I'll quit smoking just yet.

I beg of you to ask the right question

I beg of you to ask how I am

And I beg of you to care when the response is of far more information, is far more of a display of emotion, than you expected

I would merely ask this of you but this is no request

I will beg upon my knees and you will remember my words when you lie down tonight to sleep

I beg of you to care for yourself

I beg of you to alter the way you feel about the beggar

We are all beggars and the being at which we beg most is likely god

Some pretend there are many gods, some pretend there is one

Some pretend there is no god at all but I'd like to pretend that if gods exist they are the greatest celebrities of all and prefer their privacy and if no gods exist then there is little harm to come from raw belief

There is only harm to come about from our actions and the words pushed between our lips

and when harm does come of these we will accept any excuse that arises to tell ourselves what is necessary to push the day's events to the side and trade blows with the next sunrise, the next meal, the next second that passes

The young are the most immortal of the mortal that walk among us

And time, every breath, draws our life away and we should be thankful for this gift in every instant that passes as there are far worse things that can take our lives

For our lives will surely be taken

To think that what I am saying now or what will happen in the hours, days, and weeks that will proceed matter is an ideal held high among us

An ideal that drives us to preemptive decay, an ideal that slows the erosion of our misperceptions of the world around us

Don't you know we are merely the dream of a tick sucking on the flesh of the universe that is a cow awaiting slaughter?

Don't you know that this makes no sense but tugs at you slightly as surely as it tugged at me when it was written?

And now at least one of you may beg of me

Beg of me the gift of more words upon this page

Beg of me to close a wound that I may have opened

Or open a wound that was not ready to be closed

Don't you know the wisest of us know nothing but the most intelligent of us claim dearly everything we've read and learned and hold intellect before themselves as a paper costume that must not be worn out in the rain?

We tell ourselves' what we must to take what we internally insist is the proper turn at what is sometimes improbable speed

The limits are comfortable to live within and everyone including you will tell you what a good deed you've done staying within them

But to stride boldly beyond these limits resets them in others eyes so that they may fall within what you have just achieved so that you can stride boldly beyond this nonexistent boundary once again

I beg of you to know that these words of strength rise from the deepest pool of weakness and fault and I beg of you to plunge within its depths

So what is the point?

What is the point of all this madness that resides within us?

That resides within our lives

That will reside in the wake of our deaths and after

I beg of your forgiveness for I do not know

So if you find the point my friends, if you even imagine you have found a single variable in an equation that is infinite your only obligation is to share it

And this obligation will drag you through the mud and thorns of others' opinions

Opinions change

Know others are as fallible as you know yourself to be

Also know that others shape your life

I am not meant to lead. I am not meant to follow. I am meant to walk long distances alone without taking a single step

The stairs of life are endless and often the mistake is to climb as many of them as you can

Often this drives one to a breathless life

You will die in this corpse clogged stairwell

But do not be afraid

For you are meant to

Change

It's time for a change,

for the words to ascend

from this page to your mind,

slicing the chains wrapped around your enlightenment.

It's time for a change,

for the anguished look in an unfamiliar face

to mean more than crisp, cold, green slips of paper in
your pocket,

It is time for change,

for the bottom line to be drawn by that little internal
voice

you long ago stopped listening to,

instead of by your checking account balance received in
the mail.

It is time for the pen,

to gleam once again,

with a strength that is mightier than the sword.

It's time for your eyes,

so accustomed to others lies,

to see things as what they truly are for.

It's time for your mosque, your synagogue, your
chapel,

to cast away the lies of Eve and Adam's apple.

It is time to accept,

You're born flawed and inept,

and wandered through life as cattle.

It is time to cry in public without shame.

Please teach your children to weep.

We must speak publicly of personal anguish,

allowing others to know of a complete stranger's pain.

We must look at the balance of things,

at what we are losing and the fallacy of gain.

I implore you, friends, enemies,

it is time for a change.

Naive

When I was a kid

someone convinced me you could take a shit out of your mouth

I believed that Santa and the Easter bunny had some bearing on the real world

that the chicken on my plate, nearly every night, had nothing to do with

the living breathing animals I saw on television

I thought aliens built the pyramids

any animal I could catch was a pet

and

when someone asked me what I wanted to do when I grew up

I'd tell them I wanted to be an Indian

hunting buffalo on horseback

I walked for miles in the hills around my neighborhood

seeking the treasures of abandoned cars

and the unknown wealth of fossils buried just below my reach

When I was a kid

I actually found a few

Momentarily

Everyone waits for the next great

athlete

poet

American writer

for the next great

war

victory

peace

for the next not so great

morning

lunch

afternoon

sitcom

for the next

can you tell me where you have placed the present?

The instant in which we live now

Momentarily anyway

Wife to Order

He had a mail order wife

He told her to mow the lawn while he was at
work

She couldn't get the lawnmower to work

So she used a pair of scissors

Blade by blade

He thought it was the greatest thing

I dreamt I was listening to a radio station that I could
not quite tune in

I dreamt I was listening to a record that ceased to spin
whose proximity was ever changing

there was music of infinite width and depth

experimental in that it traveled many miles in my head

even as I slept I struggled to place a name upon the
sounds that I may hear them again upon awakening
from my slumber,

in my sleep this seemed attainable

I dreamt I was in a record store I had been to many
times in my dreams though I was not always welcome

I spent many hours and days in this store perusing very
little and at times held a pint of dark ale as I wandered
the aisles

I dreamt of unorthodox sound until the bottom of my
left foot began to hurt and then fall numb

I awoke with the my leg pressed against the frame of
my bed and felt as if the sole of that leg had traveled a
great distance that the rest of me had merely glimpsed

I dreamt of sound until the small cavern of my mouth
dried from within and left me to swallow painfully as I
struggled to either grasp what I heard or release the

sound from my mind that I may leave it behind

The impression left upon me is as footprints in sand

Undeniable yet undoubtedly finite

Introspective Boredom

some things never seem to pass

the ache that comes after being kicked in the balls

that asphalt stink as you pass over freshly paved road

the sting of rejection

the carrot of success

nothing

To Exist

The dirt beneath my fingernails snapped my mind

Fetching the mail was enough to make me stutter

Finding where I left the floss was enough to make me
scream

Scream almost as much as motivating myself to floss in
the first place

The growth of my fingernails seemed an impossible
feat

Going outside to smoke is at times a grave injustice

Cleaning my driver side window was a matter of
intense forethought

To remind myself of anything was an incomprehensible
task

The very act of thinking a sin

Accepting the loss of hair with age until you find a
mirror

the bathroom by the door, a journey too intense
the gift of a universal remote was crippling

I try to mark the days of note in the calendar
I try to replace the broken shoelace

I try to scrub the face and wash the hair

To change the clothes and run the machines that cleans them

To buy the stamps

to remember to ask the right questions

to give the right answers

to exist

What if God failed to evolve?

I've seen god in the separation of a cell

and I've felt god in my heart

not a cartoonish heart that grew three sizes that
Christmas day in the Grinch

but in the actual beating of my own heart

every pulse

every second passing

the muscles pressing my blood through my veins

every compression is god

but what if god failed to evolve

looking up at us with a lack of understanding

from its place

among the slime coating the ponds

within every limb of the starfish lacking

what we perceive as emotion and thought

what if god left when

our ancestors pulled themselves

webbed limb from the water

what if god lacks reasoning

only able to think as we assume

lesser animals think

as I perceive to think animals do

pursuing their instincts with

an unsullied clear mind

what if god has left our actions

what if god has left our souls to return to the life it
knows

to the life that will undoubtedly

live on after our steel turns to rust and

our piles of stone submit to the wind and the roots

what if that is god's only gift

and our only form of immortality

I sliced my hand on the screen door

It cut several inches and it was deep

I, just a kid, cried

My aunt said "Why are you crying?"

As she cleaned the wound

"You don't need to be crying"

It was then I experienced a moment of clarity

This simple statement struck me as so true that I was careful where I would place my tears from then on

I found their true value and held them more closely not out of fear or lack of comfort but because there are some things in this life that are just not worthy of my tears

Perhaps I can't find it

Perhaps I am as a blind man would be trying to find just the right photograph

Perhaps I seek the prize for days only to lie unknowingly down upon it when I need respite and awaken later to seek it out again

It may be as a set of lenses I look through in search of the very thing pressed to my face

I do not know exactly what it is that I seek and perhaps if I did I would call off the search entirely

There is the possibility that I cannot cease to seek it out until I have met the floor for one final time

The goal will not release me

 I will pursue it as surely as I will once again grow hungry

That I do not know quite what I am looking for only makes the need to look grow stronger

I tell myself I will know it when I see it and perhaps the reassurance I receive every time I repeat these words are really all I will ever find

I am not certain that I hold any desire for what I am looking for and yet at times I am so desperate to find it that little else of the world exists to me

I never really was all that good at finding things

Maybe it's one of those traits a human cannot be taught just as there are no courses offered for so many vital aspects of life

There is no school that teaches unconditional love, there is no class in which a 90% can be scored to make you content in your life, there is no tutor at the local University that can make you accept the myriad of flaws you all see in the reflection of a mirror or a mind

There is no way for me to condition myself to learn a lesson that I already know but cannot seem to apply

Perhaps if I were to just sit quietly, calmly, and with lack of care whatever it is that I cannot find will come to me.

And perhaps it will allow me to possess it, perhaps it will possess me

Perhaps whatever it is will show so much affection that I will turn it away

We All Get a Lifetime

It takes a lifetime to die

Whether this lasts for only a matter of moments

Or you are inexplicably the longest living human being
in history

In a lifetime you will die

Diagnosis

The people who really have it bad off are those who are
schizoaffective

the therapist tells my sister

A severe mood disorder combined with hearing voices
and acute paranoia

leaves them irrational,

functional cases are rare,

"Don't tell me that" my sister says my brother is
schizoaffective

I am occasionally asked how I handle it

What it is like and I pause

Briefly I ponder how to express it

When every single thought, no matter the consequence,
ripples across the top of your mind echoing tauntingly

Trying to sleep with a pillow wrapped around my head
during the quietest of nights

words not your own screaming insistently in the
background of every single day,

words not your own growing between your ears ringing
almost from behind your eyes

words not your own being silently mouthed
unconsciously, best not to let your jaw relax

Asking the technician before electroshock therapy if
anyone ever requires a small amount of current applied
to the brain regularly

Some people come back once every year or two

Asking him how many more sessions there are to go,

Asking him how many I have already had

Being asked my name, and being slow on the reply

I am occasionally asked what it is like

And I pause finding only

Words

That seem to scrape the subject raw

You get used to it.

An Idle Suffering

Think I have the answer, knowing it's not right.

spreading like a cancer screams my faltering insight.

Convinced of things, pulling the strings,

muddled thoughts that draw sharp stings.

Wallow a thousand years, drinking up my regret,

drown in an ocean, composed of my sweat.

Lie to your creator, flinching not once,

eye locked to eye, communicating in grunts.

Intermittent fallacies, latch themselves on me.

button hole sized galaxies, expanding by degree.

Ask a thousand questions then, leave without reply.

the feints, the jabs, the repartee,

Words said before they die.

clever, clever, sharp mind my device,

Seeking true courage I live with the mice.

digging a burrow with ragged bare hands.

Coaching the game from the worst seat in the stands.

screaming the answer until my throat bleeds,

With my head in a box,

none know of my deeds.

Beneficial inconsequence,

I pass among the flock.

Regurgitating chosen words,

a bloodied nursing hawk.

Questing, questing, seek the goal,

that shiny needed thing.

The years, the tears, they take their toll,

an idle suffering.

Dig

"Dig." I had spoken to him many times since we met but it was the first time I issued him a command.

"Hungry?"

"Thirsty?"

These came naturally along with our time spent together but it was the first time I had asked him a question that he might not be willing to respond to.

First I must begin the tale from the night we met and how I had decided to include my friend Dig into my quest.

There were first reports on the television, stories of regenerating dead flesh. By the time the first undead video made the airwaves the chaos in the streets had reached a climax.

It was unclear whether it was the rise of the dead that had actually sparked the massive riots or the tumultuous human response to the first afflicted corpse, but the dead had risen and the human race had been exposed to enough movies and video games to calculate that to mean that the end had come as well.

Hours before broadcast television had ceased there were images of the hordes upon the screen shot from poor angles in grainy photos, but the majority of footage consisted of very living mobs of people flipping cars and burning buildings in major cities. There was, however, one very clear shot of one of the mob, with a head wound that could be none other than fatal, lifting himself off the ground and stumbling into a pack of rioters.

All of the stations went into white noise shortly after.

To call the area my house sat in "rural" would be an understatement and to call my long dead parents "paranoid" would be as well.

They had lived their entire lives preparing to live in nearly ground zero conditions, the location of the house, the well dug on the residence, the stockpile in the basement, all these and more had been put into place specifically for the red dawn that would never arrive. When the final television channel turned to black and white particles I knew that it was sheer dumb luck that I had not sold that house decades ago and that I had holed up in it over the summer until my leg could recover.

The cottage I inherited from my father was designed for the trials I encountered when the change came, when the dead had risen. A ten foot stone wall encircled the small, one story brick home and the basement was stocked for a war that had never occurred.

When the power failed after the initial reports of the risings I sequestered myself within the basement after nailing the front door and windows shut.

It was a sentence of solitary confinement ingesting cans of green beans and endless hours of tweaking the tuner on the battery operated radio in my basement to the sounds of static.

It was during the first month I spent in the basement drinking the juice from cans that I found the meaning of solitude. The days and nights meant little in the windowless room. I would have drained the batteries from the radio long ago had there been anything to listen to. There is not a library in existence, no matter what anyone tells you, to fend off the silence of anything but your own voice, and my library was limited. The books were read and reread. The conversations I had with myself were repeated over and over.

I began to, against my better thinking, long to wander out and find what the wilderness held for me. I longed to see the sun, to grace the skyline with my eyes, or at least to peak a look from between the boards covering my front window regardless of the caution my father had instilled within me.

Then I heard someone smashing through the boards and furniture I had affixed to the front door.

I grasped my wooden cane and grabbed the one weapon I had. It was a single barrel ten gauge shotgun with a cracked wooden stock. I had eleven shells left for the gun, three of which rested within my pocket, not including the one in the chamber, and after hearing the noise coming from the floor above I decided that I would face the creature or creatures that had smashed their way into my home rather than wait complacently for them to burst through my basement door.

I hobbled up the stairs; shotgun tucked under one arm, cane supporting me with my right. I cracked the door and peaked out into the living room. I expected mobs of rotting corpses shambling through my home, but was left disappointed. The only thing I could see was the moon shining through my broken front door and the silhouette of a large man shuffling through my living room.

I opened the door slowly and dropped my cane with my right arm to hold the gun securely with my left to compensate for the kick of my shotgun.

He was fast.

Before I could take aim at the bastard my cane had hit the ground. The shadow turned quickly and slapped the shotgun to the side as I pulled the trigger. The next thing I knew was the crack of the gun, a hand clasped to my mouth and a large man pressing me to the wall.

"Shhh" was all he said, "Shhh" he repeated as he held me against the wall with one arm and pressed one finger to his mouth. He stepped away then, released my mouth from his grasp, and stood several paces from me.

It took no more convincing from me to realize that this man was not undead, given the size of him there would be little struggle if he chose to beat me to death right then and there, but he merely held the finger to his mouth for another moment, nodded, and stood back.

I bent to retrieve my cane, slowly tucked the shotgun under my free arm and opened the door to the basement motioning the man to follow me.

He nodded slightly as I motioned for him to come downstairs and walked through the door of the basement as if he'd been invited many times before. As he walked down the stairs into the light of the generator powered cellars single bulb I took stock of him.

He was at least six and a half feet tall with broad shoulders and easily over two hundred and sixty pounds. Had he wished to take what I had after pressing me against the wall of my living room and I had fired my single barrel of the shotgun he would have it. I was unsure whether I had found a much needed source of company or if I should be taking advantage of the next opportunity to reload my shotgun.

However, what struck me most was the amount of blood. The white wife beater he was wearing had not an inch of the original white and had been torn from one shoulder and clung to the other by a strand. He was covered in bite wounds all around the neck, and back and his blue denim jeans were muddy and dark. The large young man slumped into the cot I had set up in the corner and the mattress, big enough for me to lie in comfortably yet looking like a children's bed beneath him, squeaked as the springs accepted his weight and the big man lowered his head into his hands and began to shake slightly.

"Are you alone?" I began, following it up with more questions and statements that seemed to have little effect. After several more attempts at conversation that received little response besides a dead stare into his blood stained open palms. It occurred to me to take a simpler approach

"Hungry?" I said reaching for a can of pears from the shelf and holding it out in front of me.

"Hungry?" I asked again peeling the lid from the top of the container and holding it out before me. The man reached out slowly as if I were going to pull the can away at the last moment and upon taking it from me proceeded to guzzle the juice from the can, shoveling the remaining fruit into his mouth with his fingers.

As he finished the can I took stock of my present circumstances. I had bolted the door of the basement behind me. I was well aware that although it was a sturdy door it would not hold a mob of undead. Sealing the front entryway of the house with whatever I could was definitely the first thing that needed to be done.

Obviously the work I had put into barring the front door prior to the entrance of this large young man had not sufficed. It had taken the better part of a day to secure the boards to the door and move the furniture into place thanks to my reliance on a cane, and there was little light to work with as the generator was not attached to upper floors. As far as food and water I had little to be concerned with. The oversized pantry in the basement had been stocked to last a family of three at least a year and I know now that I would not have been able to exhaust this supply before being driven out into the world from the madness of isolation.

I thought of all this as I glared at the basement door at the top of the steps and finally decided that I would rely on the stone wall encircling my home to protect me until the first light of morning and then proceed to repair the damage that the man who would come to be known as Dig had done to the entrance of my home.

As the gears in my head ground on I heard a soft whine of air from my cot and glanced over to see that Dig, seated upright with his weight pressed against the wall, had fallen sound asleep, bloodied hands in his lap, eyes closed.

With my bed taken and hours from the task at hand I sat across from the stairs leading up to the basement door. I leaned over to pull the box of remaining shells close, reloaded the single barrel of my shotgun and propped it up across my good leg to wait for death or daylight.

I awoke to the sound of hammering,

Jumping from my seat, shotgun resting at my side, quite startled, I lifted myself from the ground with the aid of my cane, retrieved my weapon, and realized that Dig was no longer in the room.

The basement door lay open. I hobbled up the stairs and the view of my living room brought a smile to my face, the first time I had truly smiled since I had made the shelter beneath my house a home.

Dig had been busy.

The furniture in the living room that had been too cumbersome to move lay propped against the front doors and windows, and the remains of a large oaken bookshelf were hanging across the frame of the door by half sunken bent nails.

Dig stood before the doorway, light from the crack illuminating him as he put the hammer and nails I had left on the floor in the room to good use. His technique however needed work.

I approached Dig and he turned to me handing me the hammer and several nails with the slightest of shrugs and an expression so deadpan one would think to check for a pulse. He held the remains of the furniture close to the frame as I drove home every nail in the box.

With my home more secure than ever I motioned for Dig to return to the basement and followed him down the stairs.

There was still a matter to deal with.

Upon entering the basement Dig took his place upon the cot and gazed into his palms opening and closing them rhythmically.

Dig showed no signs of fever. I had nodded off the night before and it never occurred to me that this man would pass away in his sleep, rise from the dead, and tear me to pieces as I napped. Dig clearly bore bite wounds, but Dig was my guest. One does not turn a shotgun upon the first man he sees in a month.

I retrieved the first aid kit from a cupboard and did a quick inventory. It was less promising than I'd hoped. There were no antibiotics or pain killers, merely medical tape, a length of gauze, scissors, a bottle of alcohol, and a needle and thread.

I had to clean the wounds.

I soaked a strip of cloth in water from a torn bed sheet and approached Dig. He did not turn his head as I came forward but as I pressed the wet cloth to a gash in his shoulder he released a low growl sounding like a dog whose food was being taken mid meal.

"This won't hurt at all." I said realizing that my words were lies as they left my mouth. He stiffened as I said it and I quickly changed my tact.

"Just let me clean you up." I said as I pressed the rag to the wound in his shoulder again. He tensed every muscle in his body then and quickly grabbed my arm.

"You'll die!" I insisted, "You'll die!"

He relaxed at this and I proceeded to wipe him down beginning at his shoulders and working my way slowly down his back and chest. His back was a canvass of wounds. Some of the bites were deep and he was bruised badly across one arm, he had scratches from his shoulders to his lower back and ribs and I removed a long pointy canine from the bicep of his right arm.

He was so covered in wounds that I was tempted to simply pour alcohol across his shoulders and wipe him down once again, but the amount of pain involved might drive him to knock me across the room.

I gingerly applied an alcohol stained patch of gauze to the wounds I resolved to tape up and as the wet gauze touched his flesh he whimpered slightly. I stepped away to appraise what had been done and Dig flopped over on the cot, legs hanging from one end, sinking into a deep sleep.

I gave Dig a week within the basement of my home, feeding him and gingerly checking his bandages for infection. I spoke to him as one would a household pet, softly and with little concern that any of the contents of our conversation would go any further than the air between us. Dig proved to be as resilient as his build and appearance would appear. His deeper wounds closed with little signs of puss and his demeanor improved from staring blankly into his open palms to leaning relaxed against the walls of the basement. I took to reading to him from the novels of Mark Twain for as much my amusement as his own and though he never spoke a word it seemed to calm him.

My wife of many years had been cremated thank God, yet my daughter, who had passed at the young age of eight, lie buried in our back yard. I couldn't bear the thought of her thrashing in her casket six feet below the ground not far from where I slept for eternity. My next move had occurred to me for quite some time, a week before Dig came to me, at the time however, with my physical condition, I lacked the ability to implement any action and I had supposed that I would most likely join the ranks of the undead long before I could release her from her suffering beneath six feet of earth.

On the morning of the eighth day I rose stiffly from the floor of the basement, as I had not composed a method of removing Dig from my cot unharshly, and shook Dig from his sleep. He rose suddenly in a start and grasped my arm firmly before relaxing as he took stock of his surroundings. After Dig rose from his sleep I motioned with an underhand gesture to follow me and began to climb the stairs to the basement door. He did not follow at first, though as I reached the door and unlocked the bolt he climbed the stairs quickly behind me.

I peeked through a crack in the door and found my living room just as we'd left it, the furniture stacked in the door and windows, and the nails still holding the boards in place.

I stepped quietly into the bottom floor of my home and made my way to the back door. The back door had remained untouched from the time I had sealed it off by pushing the kitchen refrigerator against it along with a pile composed of the dining room table and chairs.

I began to drag a chair from the pile and gave a meaningful look at Dig. After a few moments he joined me in clearing the door and Dig pushed the fridge from the doorway without encouragement.

The backyard was not overly spacious. There was a lawn chair near the door and a neglected flower bed running against the side of the house as well as a small tool shed and a stack of wood along the wall. Then there was the most notable area, a large tree growing from the corner of the yard with a small simple granite tombstone beneath bearing merely the word "Grace".

"Dig." I said to him after scratching out a large rectangular line in the dirt before my daughter Grace's tombstone. I crossed the yard to the shovel I'd pulled from the shed and hobbled over to the center of the plot, jammed the business end of the shovel into the dirt and repeated, "Dig".

At that moment I made the decision to forever refer to the young man as "Dig".

True to his namesake Dig carved the dirt from the earth six feet by four feet, and as the sun began to set he had nearly reached the casket of my beloved daughter.

I had no knowledge as to exactly how deep Grace's casket lay or the length and the width of the coffin however I was made aware by the noise of my dear undead daughter thrashing within her box. The noise was muted by the wooden lid of her coffin and masked at first by the sounds of shoveling from my one companion Dig, but as Dig stopped to catch his breath and the digging ceased for a moment it was clear that Grace had found new life at the bottom of her hole.

Dig shoveled till the lid of the casket lay bare and after a glance over his shoulder to me began to thrust the tip of the shovel into wooden casket, prying at the seam of the edges of the box.

"No!" I said as soon as I heard the boards of the coffin creak. "No!"

"Come out of the hole!" I demanded and Dig looked up surprised to hear it after coming so close to the supposed prize

"Get out of there." I barked and Dig slowly pulled himself out of the hole he had created.

I did not have much gasoline remaining from the drum in the basement but I suppose that I could spare a few gallons to ease the suffering of my only dear child.

"We have to burn her, Dig." I limped my way to the wood pile and tucked two cut chunks of wood beneath my free arm.

Dig made two trips to the woodpile filling his arms with split logs and tossing them down the hole.

After the lid of the casket lay covered in hunks of wood I soaked an old shirt in gasoline, emptied the remainder into the grave, lit the cloth, and watched the last resting place of my dear daughter Grace burn.

I, as well as Dig, added wood to the pile several times a few logs at a time. The pile shifted at one point but I never saw even a fingertip of my deceased daughter.

I do not know how I would have gone on if I had.

The day passed. The bed of coals cooled. Dig and I had looked down silently as we watched the fire take its course.

As the sun was setting Dig looked up meaningfully at me with his knuckles gripping the shovel sticking from the ground and I nodded.

Dig did not so much as grunt as he silently filled the grave of my daughter with shovelful after shovelful of dirt.

The dirt was smoothed out over her grave. Dig did one final pat of the shovel onto the freshly dug earth then he took the shovel firmly in both hands. Drove it into the loose soil and said softly as he looked directly into my eyes.

"I had a son…"

The Land Rover was loaded before dawn in silence. There was no discussion of what we needed, I merely pointed at a box of canned goods or motioned to some flares and Dig quietly packed it away into the car.

I limped to the iron gate blocking the garage and stood in silence taking a long look at the world outside into the trees surrounding my home. I heard only birds and the rustle of pine needles in the wind.

I walked slowly to the open garage as Dig did some final adjustments to the supplies packed in the back of the SUV. Dig closed the back of the car and approached me without a word and, with a questioning look, held his empty hand out before me. I placed the keys into his palm and he closed his hand over them. He then reached out to me with his other arm and firmly squeezed my shoulder. He silently opened the gate and climbed into the vehicle as I limped around to the passenger side.

I climbed in and placed the shotgun between us and Dig started the car. We pulled out slowly onto the dirt road and I turned the tuner of the radio left and right across the bandwidth. There was one station broadcasting and R.E.M. blared out "It's the end of the world as we know it and I feel fine." I leaned forward, tense, waiting for a news broadcast but the song repeated itself once and then again.

Dig drove slowly down the road until it became gravel and after the fifth repeat of the song he reached over and switched the radio off.

Dig seemed to know every turn and soon we were driving down the middle of a narrow road.

We slowly came upon a car half slid into a ditch on our right. Dig accelerated the vehicle but as we passed I got a decent look.

The driver side window and windshield were nearly shattered and dark red with dried blood. The passenger side door was wide open but there was no movement

Dig drove only on the back roads for an hour there was little to see but a trail of smoke rising in the east.

We passed a large field of flowers on our right shortly after and as I looked out upon a sea of dandelions I saw the silhouette of a man standing in the field with his both arms held out from his sides and his face held to the sun.

I looked to see if Dig had seen this as well but Dig only glanced through the side window and once again accelerated.

I had expected hordes of the undead, roads clogged with cars and bands of road warriors, but instead I received a fairly quiet drive. The back road we were on turned to thin gravel and led up a green hillside into a small cemetery. It was merely a plot of graves.

Dig pulled the car up to the end of the road, turned it off, and handed me the keys. I held them in my hand silently as Dig looked straight ahead through the wind shield, sighed, opened the door and we prepared for the dig.

There was no one in sight. Dig led me straight to the grave without hesitation carrying a shovel in hand and a gallon of gas in the other. I had the shotgun tucked under one arm and a back pack filled with supplies.

It was a small graveyard covering the top of the hillside. All of the markers were fairly modest. Some of the tombstones were mere stumps of rotting wood and most were flat slabs of carved granite set low in the ground. When we reached the grave I thought surely that I would have some hint of at least a family name for Dig but there was merely a wooden cross sticking from the earth with "Bobby" carved across it.

As we reached the grave the shovel and gas Dig was carrying were dropped to the ground and Dig stood silently clasping and unclasping his hands at his sides staring into the dirt. I let my cane drop at my side and held the shotgun in both hands taking a long look around me at the peaceful valley surrounding us.

I then looked to Dig. His face remained blank and his stare remained fixed at the ground at the foot of the wooden cross. I knew many answers lay there. I knew then that the silence of what may be my only friend was held six feet below and I had little doubt that this is exactly where it would remain. Dig would never tell his story. Perhaps I may one day get more than four words from him, but it was very likely that he was the only living human being with the knowledge of why he remained silent and it was very likely that he would take this knowledge to his grave.

I stood quietly for some time watching Dig stare at the grave clenching and unclenching his hands. Finally my leg began to grow sore. I picked the cane up from the ground and, limping around the grave I dragged my cane through the dirt in front of the marker six feet long and four feet wide.

I stood across the lines from my friend, giving him one more moment to his thoughts and then merely said "Dig."

Dig retrieved the shovel and did just that. The shovel entered the earth, came back filled, was flipped over the shoulder and stuck back into the earth again and again. He did not pause to catch his breath, or even wipe the sweat from his face.

The hole grew from a dent in the ground to a shallow pit until soon the ground around him had risen over his shoulders.

As he dug closer and closer to the casket the moaning, growling and scratching of his dead son grew clearer and clearer and his pace increased until the pine box was cleared of the dirt.

His son had been strong. The lid of the coffin remained on the casket but the kicking and clawing shook the box just enough to stir the dust from its surface.

All the while I stood in place, shotgun in hand, watching Dig work, watching the tree lines at the bottom of the hill for movement and the passing of the sun across the sky.

Dig threw the shovel to the side, pulled himself from the hole, and marched off into the woods. I watched quietly as he came back minutes later dragging an armful of branches and jammed them into the hole. Three more times he marched off into the woods returning with dead logs and armfuls of sticks until a pile of wood covered his son's casket.

Dig then emptied most of the can of gas onto the wood and I silently handed him a flare.

As the flames lit the night Dig stared into them for a time and then sat, exhausted, and watched fire rise from the grave.

I hobbled over to him. Took a seat next to him, loaded shotgun at my side, and pulled a flask from my pack.

"Fifty year old scotch" I said as I passed the flask to him. He took a long pull and handed it back. "No" I said "After my daughter's death not even the end of the world could drive me to take another drink." He patted me on the back then and drank more.

As Dig made his way through the flask of scotch I could see the tension fall from his shoulders. I began to talk. I talked of the random things that would come up in conversation at any random bar on a random day. I talked to him about the first woman I had ever loved. I talked to him about the first time I was ever arrested. Eventually I began to tell jokes looking out over those flames as Dig grew drunk.

All the while the tension from his face fell and flask was tipped back.

"You know you'd be a great action hero in a silent movie." I finally said and when I looked from the flames to his face I saw the just the slightest of smiles.

"Could I borrow a shovel?" The question came from a gravelly voice across the flames and I looked up to see a figure lit by the fire.

I began to go for the shotgun but the figure sat across from us in the glow and said "There's no need for that. I won't hurt you. My name's Greg."

"What brings you out here, Greg?" I asked casually keeping one hand on the shotgun and peering out into the night behind him.

"I suppose I'm here for the same reason as you two, to visit the dead, says a lot about the god that created us that the dead would come back in such a way, tearing at the lives of the living. Hell of a way to return. Not really what one would think of when they think of a second coming."

I tucked the shotgun closer and reached into the pack at my side for a flashlight. Dig, clearly a little drunk, held the flask out before him, offering the man a drink.

"Thanks but no thanks I have no use for that any longer. You know the after life is nothing as I had imagined it. There were no clouds filled with loved ones just death and then a terrible hunger. Still it is nice once the hunger passes and your mind returns. I have no need in existence except to rot away peacefully and enjoy the last days of my former species."

I pulled the light free and shined it all around but there was no one to be seen but this man. Finally I placed the light on him again and looked closer.

"There is always loneliness I suppose. Even the dead need company. Honestly I'm not sure how many of us will ever cease to embody nothing but hunger. After time I was just no longer hungry. It is too bad that none of us were ever truly created to be alone. I suppose god tired of our little rat race and decided it was time for a change. I hate to bother the two of you but could I use your shovel? My families plot is at the bottom of the hill."

I stood and threw more gas on the flames for a better look. He appeared to be more or less intact for a dead man. There was a yellowish color to his face and he had chewed away some of his own lips. He had a hole in his chest that glistened in the fire but other than that he looked pretty good for a corpse.

Dig stood, walked around the fire, and handed the man the shovel. "Dig" he said with a smile.

The world had always been an uncertain place. The end of it now seemed even more uncertain. It seemed the best I could do was to die a lame old man in good company.

We left Greg there with the shovel that night digging away in the dark without much else to say. He had no answers. Who can honestly say that they do?

Dig stood a chance I suppose, a tough young man like that silent in the face of horror and possessing such strength.

So what now?

There was only one gas station in the area but half a tank full would get us to the most beautiful scenic view I have ever seen. One last thing of great beauty before rolling the dice and wandering into the burning world out there, it was more than my daughter received and most likely Bobby as well.

Besides I could use some good conversation.

The Last Masterpiece

I admire the edge

Razor sharp

Many little teeth tearing at my skin as I run my fingertip across them

I grasp the plastic handle in my palms

Looking down upon the blade as its point dimples my stomach

I jam the knife into my belly and pull to the side

My innards spill out

All the beautiful colors of my guts

Onto the table

Onto the blank sheets of paper I've placed there

So slowly dying

I arrange my intestines

Smearing the art of my insides from page to page

My final work

Undeniably defined

Index

www.ingramcontent.com/pod-product-compliance
Lightning Source LLC
Chambersburg PA
CBHW061820040426

42447CB00012B/2744